# At Odds in the World
## Essays on Jewish Canadian Women Writers

# At Odds in the World
## Essays on Jewish Canadian Women Writers

Ruth Panofsky

INANNA Publications and Education nc.
Toronto, Canada

Copyright © 2008 Ruth Panofsky

Except for the use of short passages for review purposes, no part of this book may be reproduced, in part or in whole, or transmitted in any form or by any means, electronically or mechanically, including photocopying, recording, or any information or storage retrieval system, without prior permission in writing from the publisher.

  Canada Council   Conseil des Arts
 for the Arts    du Canada

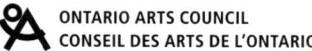

We gratefully acknowledge the support of the Canada Council for the Arts and the Ontario Arts Council for our publishing program.

We are also grateful for the support received from an Anonymous Fund at The Calgary Foundation.

Cover design: Val Fullard
Cover artwork: J. T. Winik, "Trinity," detail, oil on canvas, 31.5" x 23", 2003
Interior design: Luciana Ricciutelli

Library and Archives Canada Cataloguing in Publication

Panofsky, Ruth
   At odds in the world : essays on Jewish Canadian women writers / Ruth Panofsky.

Includes bibliographical references and index.
ISBN 978-0-9808822-4-7

   1. Canadian prose literature (English)—Women authors—History and criticism. 2. Canadian prose literature (English)—Jewish authors—History and criticism. 3. Jewish women in literature.  4. Group identity in literature.
I. Title.

PS8089.5.J4P36 2008     C818'.540809287     C2008-906040-7

Printed and bound in Canada

Inanna Publications and Education Inc.
210 Founders College, York University
4700 Keele Street
Toronto, Ontario, Canada M3J 1P3
Telephone: (416) 736-5356 Fax (416) 736-5765
Email: inanna@yorku.ca

*For Liza, my loving daughter*

# Table of Contents

Acknowledgements ix

Introduction 1

1. "This Problem of Identity": Miriam Waddington's *Summer at Lonely Beach and Other Stories* 13

2. "Ambiguity and Paradox": A Conversation with Helen Weinzweig 33

3. A "Sense of Loss": The Fiction of Helen Weinzweig 45

4. Close to the Bone: Woman's Place in Nora Gold's *Marrow and Other Stories* 61

5. From Complicity to Subversion: The Female Subject in Adele Wiseman's Novels 73

6. "This Was Her Punishment": Jew, Whore, Mother in the Fiction of Adele Wiseman and Lilian Nattel 83

7.
"The Freedom to Write": The Memoirs of Fredelle Bruser
Maynard and Joyce Maynard     98

Index     113

# Acknowledgements

I am indebted to Danielle Deveau and Michael Green for invaluable research assistance, to reference librarian Felicity Pickup, Robarts Library, University of Toronto for expert advice, and to Annette Zilversmit for referring me to The Maimie Papers. I have had the honour of co-supervising the doctoral research of Julie Spergel, who shares my scholarly interest in the fiction of Jewish Canadian women writers. A number of colleagues have read and commented on earlier versions of these essays. I would like to thank Sylvia Brown, Laura McLauchlan, Andrea O'Reilly, Liz Podnieks, and Lois E. Rubin for their incisive and helpful suggestions toward improving the essays in this collection. To my editor, Luciana Ricciutelli, I owe the deepest gratitude for her inspiring interest in my work and heartfelt encouragement.

Several of these essays first appeared in *Atlantis*, *Canadian Literature*, *Connections and Collisions: Identities in Jewish American Women's Writing*, and the *Journal of the Association for Research on Mothering*.

# Introduction

> [The writer] who seeks to challenge and transform the conflicted matrix of diaspora, Judaism, Jewish American identity, and womanhood into a narrative vision of heroic selfhood is still at sea.
> —Miriyam Glazer ("Daughters" 94)

Although she refers specifically to Jewish American writers, critic Miriyam Glazer's comment also applies to Canadian writers who probe women's lives as they are framed and shaped by the patriarchal culture and practice of Judaism. Like Jewish Americans who have suffered "because they were women, and because they were writers" (Walden 1), Jewish Canadian women have written to "inscribe an experience of existential displacement and exile, of 'Otherness' as sources of anguish and anger" (Glazer, "Orphans" 128). Unlike their American sisters, however—with the notable exception of prominent novelists Adele Wiseman (1928-1992) and Anne Michaels (1958- )—writing by Jewish Canadian women has received little critical attention. Michael Greenstein, a leading scholar of Jewish Canadian literature, has admitted that while twentieth century "Jewish-American novelists and poets were well served by a host of Jewish critics who interpreted their work to a vast reading public, no similar critical mediation occurred in Canada where a diminished audience and belated cultural history created a relative vacuum" (5) for Jewish authors. Hence, in the absence of a Jewish Canadian critical tradition, this volume seeks to situate the prose of Miriam Waddington, Adele Wiseman, Helen

Weinzweig, Fredelle Bruser Maynard, Joyce Maynard, Nora Gold, and Lilian Nattel within the broad parameters of writing by Jewish women in North America.

The writers examined here continue the interrogation of Jewish women's experience, begun earlier by immigrant women to Canada who wrote fiction and poetry in their mother tongue of Yiddish. Their lives changed dramatically during the twentieth century, and English gradually displaced Yiddish as the language of publication, but the fiction of Nora Gold, for instance, shows that Jewish Canadian women writers, like the American writers Glazer has studied, feel fragmented still, at "home neither in time nor in space, of unanchored personal identity" (Glazer, "Orphans" 131).

This volume brings together a series of scholarly essays that reflect my career-long interest in writing by Jewish Canadian women, in particular work that is situated at the margins of literary and Jewish studies. Although each piece was conceived and written for a particular occasion, collectively the essays show a consistent engagement with issues of cultural identity, specifically how female Jewish identity is constructed in Canadian prose works that span the years 1956 to 2004. That Jewish American women writers have been the subject of recent critical study signals the rise in the United States of scholarly investigation of race, ethnicity, and faith, and the intersection of these categories with those of gender, sexuality, and class.[1] The essays gathered here are a result of this heightened interest in Jewish women writers initiated by American critics—one of the more fortuitous effects of the rise of Jewish Studies programs in universities across North America. As the first volume to focus exclusively on writing by Jewish Canadian women, this collection aims to deepen and broaden the scholarly canvas, to situate key representative works within a North American critical paradigm of Jewish literary studies. As a collection of essays, however, this book does not seek to develop a single, overarching argument; rather, the essays that follow are eclectic in perspective and approach and represent a range of scholarly concerns.

My own gendered and cultural identity has fueled an abiding scholarly interest in female writers whose work has not reached a wide readership or enjoyed the critical attention accorded their male colleagues. One such example in contrasts is that of novelists Mordecai Richler and Adele Wiseman. During his lifetime, Richler was highly regarded for his incomparable depiction of Jewish Montreal and following his death in 2001 his work has remained popular with readers and critics alike. In contrast, Wiseman, who died in 1992, less prolific than her literary peer but whose work is no less accomplished, never shared Richler's popular or critical success.

My earliest efforts to explore my Jewish heritage through contemporary literary works, first as an adolescent and then as an undergraduate student, led me to Richler's oeuvre. Although I appreciated Richler's depiction of a full and vital world—the dynamic St. Urbain Street of my own parents' childhood and youth—I was troubled by his unflattering depiction of Jewish women. My search for contemporary writers who might counter Richler's negative characterization finally uncovered the poetry of Miriam Waddington and the prose of Adele Wiseman. As a university student seeking literary articulation of a cultural identity that often felt uncomfortable and constricting, I was cheered by my discovery of two women writers who might offer inspiration and clarification. Waddington and Wiseman inspired me—I later wrote my Masters Research Paper on Waddington's early poetry and have since published widely on the life and work of Adele Wiseman—but comprehending the complex cultural positioning of Jewish women in literature would remain elusive for many years.

It was as a graduate student that my scholarly interest in writing by Jewish Canadian women began to take formal shape, nurtured by my burgeoning desire to bridge intellectual ambition and a private preoccupation with the matter of cultural identity. In the 1980s, when I entered graduate school, I was exposed to the feminist criticism of Rachel Blau DuPlessis, Sandra M. Gilbert, Susan Gubar, and Nancy K. Miller, for example, whose work was influencing the literary examination of ethnicity and race. To my reading of works by Jewish Canadian women—a series of literary works that had expanded considerably following my discovery of Waddington and Wiseman—I brought a self-conscious Jewish identity, a feminist awareness, and a penchant for literary analysis. That my professors sanctioned my intention to probe the articulation of Jewishness and femaleness through the lens of literature helped consolidate my scholarly direction.

This volume focuses on prose works. Although the critical path first led me to Miriam Waddington's poetry, my literary scholarship on Jewish Canadian women has since concentrated on prose, including fiction, creative non-fiction, and life writing. In extended prose works, which can delineate complete worlds in ways not possible in poetry, I have continually mined my preoccupation with cultural identity to unearth a literary portrait of how it feels to be Jewish, Canadian, and female in a world that is often hostile and unaccommodating. Indeed, as I worked to assemble the essays in this volume, I noted similarities of form across the texts under consideration. I also was struck by thematic consistencies that prompted me to prepare this very collection.

These essays are intended to introduce readers to lesser known writers and to widen the traditional English-language literary canon, which comprises Miriam Waddington, Adele Wiseman, and Anne Michaels, but few other Jewish Canadian women. Of the seven authors represented here—Waddington, Wiseman, Helen Weinzweig, Fredelle Bruser Maynard and her daughter Joyce Maynard, Nora Gold, and Lilian Nattel—two were born outside of Canada. Although she was born in Poland, Weinzweig immigrated to this country as a young girl and spent her formative years in Toronto. Joyce Maynard, born and raised in the United States during her mother's extended residency in New Hampshire, retained links to Fredelle Bruser Maynard's country of origin through regular visits to family relations. Hence, unlike other Jewish authors who emigrated to Canada later in life, in the early years of the twentieth century, after the First World War, or in the terrible wake of the Holocaust, the authors discussed in this volume—with the exception of Joyce Maynard—write as Canadians, out of a deep, intuitive understanding of their homeland. Theirs is not a nationalist project, however. Instead, each writer seeks to investigate the intersecting complexities of her identity as a Canadian, a Jew, and a woman, and to critique prevailing notions, for example, of Canada as a country that embraces people of all faiths, of Judaism as open to female participation, and of Jewish women as submissive within marriage.

Many of these writers experiment with narrative form. Often, they eschew the linear constrictions of the realistic mode in favour of a liberating fragmentation and discursiveness that allows them to posit unfamiliar plot trajectories for their transgressive characters. In order, for example, to accommodate the larger-than-life figures of Hoda and Nehama Korzen, the Jewish prostitutes who dominate Adele Wiseman's *Crackpot* and Lilian Nattel's *The Singing Fire*, respectively, it is necessary to dismantle linear narrative practices that aim to contain and delimit fictional opportunities for women. The linguistic density of Wiseman's novel is intended to accommodate Hoda's garrulousness and girth, and Nattel's fragmented narrative mirrors the dislocations and disruptions of Nehama's life. To retain the shimmer of ambiguity that lies at the heart of her short fiction, Miriam Waddington eschews resolution in favour of open endings. For Helen Weinzweig, the only way to accurately represent contemporary Jewish marriage is through the juxtaposition and collision of abstract narrative vignettes that, taken together, expose a hollow institution. That same hollowness is felt by many of Nora Gold's protagonists whose barren relationships and thwarted desires to participate in religious practice are rendered through spare language and bare images. Fredelle Bruser Maynard and Joyce Maynard prefer the form of the memoir to prose fiction to articulate their respective feelings of ambivalence as Jewish mother and daughter and their sense of dissociation from home and culture.

Form is not the sole vehicle, however, through which these authors foreground cultural issues. Their thematic concerns also show a deep cultural engagement. In her introduction to *Canadian Jewish Short Stories*, editor Miriam Waddington outlines several themes that preoccupy Canadian Jewish writers: "the continuity of a Jewish tradition containing religion, ethics, and culture that includes two languages besides English and French—namely Yiddish and Hebrew"; "the individual's sense of belonging to a marginal group and being part of that collective"; "the knowledge that always, in some other place on this earth, distant or near, Jews are being oppressed and persecuted"; and "exile and problems of uncertain or divided identity" (xii). Waddington adds, "Jewish writing always has a moral dimension, and nearly always reflects the age-old quest for knowledge" (xiii).

In the essays that follow, I argue—both explicitly and implicitly—that the authors represented here examine the faith, ethics, and culture of Judaism, and show the idiomatic impact of Yiddish on English. They situate their protagonists at the margins of dominant society and their own cultural community. Their work is rooted in a history of persecution; and they write out of a compelling need to reconcile their fractured identities as Jews, Canadians, and women. More significant is the moral tenor of their work and their protagonists' quests for knowledge, both self-knowledge and communal understanding. The distinguishing feature of their work, however, significantly absent from Waddington's invaluable assessment, is its feminist orientation. Indeed, it was the authors' feminist approach to Jewish matters that drew me to the prose works I discuss in this volume. After much time spent reading the work of Jewish writers, both male and female, my efforts were rewarded: I had located Canadian works inflected by a powerful Jewish feminism, works that question the patriarchal practices and world-view of traditional Judaism.

It did not surprise me to learn that gender identity is of paramount concern to the authors whose work is covered here. What I did not anticipate, however, was each writer's open, often daring contestation of conventional gender roles for women within Judaism. Whether it is a bold flouting of gender roles—a woman's decision to lead prayers in the synagogue in Gold's story "The Prayer," for example—or a less subversive act—a daughter-in-law who challenges her father-in-law's authoritative point of view in Wiseman's novel *The Sacrifice*—each author seeks to probe and problematize the customary, secondary position of women within Judaism. Moreover, that these new articulations of female experience remain true to the moral imperative of Jewish writing and are undertaken in the interest of self-knowledge—to return to two key features of Jewish Canadian writing identified by Waddington—attests to each author's respect for and valuing of her cultural inheritance.

In addition to gender identity, a number of common themes link these authors' works. Each is deeply concerned with woman's place within Judaism, for example, as an observant member of a congregation, an unobservant member of the Jewish community, or a wife and mother in a traditional Jewish marriage. As these writers show, Judaism—at once a faith and a culture—is not monotholic and it serves women in ways both positive and negative. Each protagonist struggles to negotiate a place for herself within Judaism. The arduous process of negotiation that requires a woman's self-conscious determination is borne out by each work.

Judaism's emphasis on the role of women in the family means that each protagonist is defined by her relationships with others. The centrality of marriage to a woman's life; the relationship between wife and husband; the wife and mother as communal gatekeeper; the influence of mothers on daughters; the attachment of girls and women to their mothers, sisters, female relatives and friends—these recurring themes signal the degree to which women are conceived as pivotal figures within the Jewish community, keepers of the faith and the familial hearth, and each writer's need to excavate the cultural impact of their prescribed role within the family.

Another recurring theme is female sensuality in its myriad forms—both within and outside marriage—female sexuality as liberating or stifling, a source of fulfillment or dissatisfaction; childbirth; miscarriage; barrenness; and, perhaps most striking, prostitution. In the works under consideration, the degree to which a protagonist is free to express her sexuality is one measure of the degree of her communal acceptance. The essays in this volume recognize female sexuality as an important vehicle through which each author asserts her view of a woman's place within Judaism. The fact that female sexuality emerges so clearly as a central literary concern can be linked to its significance within Judaism itself where sexual expression, for men and women, is sanctioned within marriage, so long as it conforms to regulating patriarchal codes of behaviour.

The opening essay on Miriam Waddington, the first to study her short stories, includes a profile of the author and is intended to widen and deepen the current understanding of her literary oeuvre. Throughout her career, Waddington wrote prose alongside poetry and used the medium of fiction to investigate the conflicted position of adolescent and adult women as Jews and Canadians. Her stories, meticulously crafted and elegantly nuanced, are powerful articulations of the thematic concerns she outlines so clearly in her critical introduction to *Canadian Jewish Short Stories*.

The two companion pieces on Helen Weinzweig, an interview conducted in Toronto in 1998 and an overview of her oeuvre, profile a lesser-known author and the depth and range of her literary vision. The essay is intended to introduce readers to a uniquely talented writer whose experimental narrative technique and dark perspective has not won her the recognition she deserves. A voracious reader throughout her life, Weinzweig began her writing career at the late age of forty-five and to date has published two novels and one collection of short stories. The polish and maturity of her prose is the happy result of her literary acuity, sense of focus, and determination to see her work in print. In her fiction, Weinzweig attends to the experience of married women and their sense of malaise in relationships that stifle their autonomy and creative potential.

Nora Gold, author of a volume of short stories, shares Weinzweig's interest in the desolation of women in unsatisfying relationships. Gold's narratives, whose settings are the most contemporary of the works discussed here, are bleak in their depictions of women who are alienated from their Jewish roots, their families, and their romantic partners. In story after story, Gold charts the demise of personal relationships and a woman's gradual descent into dejection. Faith and family offer little succour to women who are unmoored. Their lack of connection is often the result of having been betrayed by their religion, or by the very men who are in a position to offer the support they require, a dilemma shared by Weinzweig's protagonists.

The essay on Adele Wiseman's two novels, *The Sacrifice* (1956) and *Crackpot* (1974), derives from my earlier work on an annotated bibliography of Wiseman's oeuvre, published in 1992.[2] The bibliography required that I read and annotate all primary and secondary material pertaining to Wiseman, an experience that led to a deep appreciation for her work. In this feminist reading of Wiseman's novels, I argue that *Crackpot* functions as a revisionist text, written against *The Sacrifice* as an attempt to seek retribution for the seductress Laiah's death. The essay brings a fresh approach to Wiseman's novels—both texts are the subject of substantive criticism—and foregrounds their preoccupation with sexual identity, a common concern in the works studied here.

The sixth essay returns to the subject of female sexuality and offers a focused analysis of the prostitute/mother as an unsanctioned figure in Wiseman's *Crackpot* and Lilian Nattel's *The Singing Fire*. The Jewish prostitute, I argue, is condoned while she serves a necessary communal function; once she acts autonomously and dares to become a mother, however, she forfeits communal acceptance and is made to endure severe punishment. The subject of female sexuality, one of the themes that unify the essays gathered here, becomes an important vehicle to elucidate woman's place within Judaism.

The final essay analyzes the respective memoirs of Fredelle Bruser Maynard and Joyce Maynard as works of life writing that, taken together, underscore the seminal importance of the mother-daughter relationship. This essay focuses on the complex connection between a mother/writer and daughter/student. In this case, the mother serves as a professional mentor to her daughter whom she trains for a career in writing. For Fredelle—who married outside her faith and whose cultural ties to Judaism lessened over time—faith and culture are displaced by mentoring as the primary means of nurturing her daughter's individual identity. The essay probes the intimate revelations offered in their memoirs to uncover an unresolved tension between mother and daughter. Through their respective identity struggles as daughters, wives, mothers, and writers, each woman comes to a heightened understanding of their relationship, and a new appreciation for her individuality and connection to Judaism, the locus of which, for the Maynards, is the traditional bond between mother and child. That the act of writing facilitates this reconciliation is not lost on either mother or daughter.

The theme of familial relationships gives way finally to a pervasive ambivalence articulated as a deeply rooted conflict felt by Jewish female characters at odds in the world, with themselves, and their identity. Waddington's reference to an "uncertain or divided identity" (xii) applies to the female protagonists examined in this volume, women who respond to their situations with a range of opposing emotions—resistance and resignation, joy and anger, love and hatred. Nonetheless, they retain an abiding desire to be part of the very community that often shuns or marginalizes them; that they continually seek communal integration and acceptance speaks to the value they attach to their cultural inheritance. Although the legacy of that inheritance is never easy, as each protagonist discovers and her creator asserts, abandonment of one's cultural roots—even for Fredelle Bruser Maynard and Joyce Maynard—is never considered. The result is a series of works that evoke, both separately and together, a disturbing paradox that can lead, but briefly, to reconciliation. It is the lack of resolution that stands as one of the more powerful reasons to study the works under consideration in this book: while they do not proffer solutions, they open outward toward fruitful, provocative discussion.

## Notes

[1]See, for example, Evelyn Avery's edited volume, *Modern Jewish Women Writers in America*; Janet Burstein, *Writing Mothers, Writing Daughters: Tracing the Maternal in Stories by American Jewish Women*; Alyse Fisher Roller, *The Literary Imagination of Ultra-Orthodox Jewish Women: An Assessment of a Writing Community*; Lois E. Rubin, ed., *Connections and Collisions: Identities in Contemporary Jewish-American Women's Writing*; Ann R. Shapiro, Sara R. Horowitz, Ellen Schiff, and Miriyam Glazer, eds., *Jewish American Women Writers: A Bio-Bibliographical and Critical Sourcebook*; and Jay L. Halio and Ben Siegel, eds., *Daughters of Valor: Contemporary Jewish American Women Writers*.
[2]See Ruth Panofsky, *Adele Wiseman: An Annotated Bibliography*.

## Works Cited

Avery, Evelyn, ed. *Modern Jewish Women Writers in America*. New York: Palgrave Macmillan, 2007.
Burstein, Janet. *Writing Mothers, Writing Daughters: Tracing the Maternal in Stories by American Jewish Women*. Urbana: University of Illinois Press, 1996.

Glazer, Miriyam. "'Daughters of Refugees of the Ongoing-Universal-Endless-Upheaval': Anne Roiphe and the Quest for Narrative Power in Jewish American Women's Fiction." *Daughters of Valor: Contemporary Jewish American Women Writers*. Eds. Jay L. Halio and Ben Siegel. Newark: University of Delaware Press, 1997. 80-96.

Glazer, Miriyam. "Orphans of Culture and History: Gender and Spirituality in Contemporary Jewish-American Women's Novels." *Tulsa Studies in Women's Literature* 13.1 (Spring 1994): 127-41.

Greenstein, Michael. *Third Solitudes: Tradition and Discontinuity in Jewish-Canadian Literature*. Montreal: McGill-Queen's University Press, 1989.

Halio, Jay L., and Ben Siegel, eds. *Daughters of Valor: Contemporary Jewish American Women Writers*. Newark: University of Delaware Press, 1997.

Panofsky, Ruth. *Adele Wiseman: An Annotated Bibliography*. Toronto: ECW Press, 1992.

Roller, Alyse Fisher. *The Literary Imagination of Ultra-Orthodox Jewish Women: An Assessment of a Writing Community*. Jefferson, NC: McFarland, 1999.

Rubin, Lois E., ed. *Connections and Collisions: Identities in Contemporary Jewish-American Women's Writing*. Newark: University of Delaware Press, 2005.

Shapiro, Ann R., Sara R. Horowitz, Ellen Schiff, and Miriyam Glazer, eds. *Jewish American Women Writers: A Bio-Bibliographical and Critical Sourcebook*. Westport: Greenwood Press, 1994.

Waddington, Miriam, ed. Introduction. *Canadian Jewish Short Stories*. Ed. M. Waddington. Toronto: Oxford University Press, 1990. xi-xvii.

Walden, Daniel. "Jewish Women Writers and Women in Jewish Literature: An Introduction." *Studies in American Jewish Literature* 3 (1983): 1-5.

# 1.
# "This Problem of Identity"

Miriam Waddington's *Summer at Lonely Beach and Other Stories*

Although she is known primarily as a poet, Miriam Waddington also wrote and published short stories. *Summer at Lonely Beach and Other Stories* (1982) assembles fourteen of Waddington's stories, written between 1940 and 1980, that reflect the spare, elegant style of her poetry and its insistent probing of personal and cultural identity, specifically her Jewish, Canadian, and Russian heritage; the fragile nature of human relationships; and the impact of geography on the writer's imagination. Strikingly, even more so than her poetry, Waddington's prose is deeply concerned with Jewish identity, especially as it pertains to women. Throughout her volume of stories, many of which explore the diverse experiences of female protagonists, Jewish identity is foregrounded as complicated and difficult, particularly as it is shaped and influenced by Canadian citizenship. Invariably, Waddington's female characters feel doubly marginalized, uncertain of their place within Judaism and outsiders in Canada where, alienated and estranged from religious, cultural, and national roots, they feel "the inconsolable strangeness of this transplanted landscape halfway between Europe and North America" (*Summer* 29). This essay reads Waddington's stories through a diasporic, layered lens of personal identity to show how issues of culture, ethnicity, and citizenship intersect repeatedly only to shade into irresolution. In stories that deliberately eschew closure and end regularly "on the brink of something new" (*Summer* 30), Waddington's female characters remain unmoored, their cultural locations unclear, and their personal identities fragmented.

Miriam Dworkin was born on 23 December 1917 in Winnipeg,

Manitoba and was raised in the city's North End, a vibrant enclave of Jewish, Polish, and Ukrainian immigrants and one-time centre of Jewish life in the West. Today, Winnipeg's North End enjoys the same legendary status as St. Urbain Street in Montreal, immortalized in large part by novelist Mordecai Richler as the former Jewish heart of that city. Dworkin's father had emigrated from Russia to Canada in 1907 or 1908; her parents met and married in Winnipeg where her father opened a sausage-making and meat-curing factory. Isidore Dworkin and Mussia Dobrusin were secular Jews, "deeply involved in the vivid intellectual life of Winnipeg's Russian Jewish community" (Moritz 5). They may not have attended synagogue, but their circle of friends and acquaintances included Jewish and Yiddish writers and lecturers, poets, musicians, and actors, some of whom were Zionists, socialists, and anarchists (Moritz 5). Waddington herself explained:

> My parents made a conscious effort that we should speak only Yiddish at home, because they felt like many secular Jews that a language was a culture ... a spiritual home. So my parents felt that language was very important, and since they were not religious they perhaps transferred their religious feelings to the language and literature and to the Yiddish culture. I think it must have been my first language. (qtd. in Binder 83-84)

Waddington attended the Peretz School, a small, permissive Yiddish-language school where literature was taught as an important subject and her nascent love of poetry was nurtured.

Waddington's childhood and youth were characterized by tension between her inner and outer lives. She once admitted that her "inner life, my really freer life was the one I had in the Jewish parochial school" (qtd. in Binder 83), which she attended until grade four. In 1927, she left the protective atmosphere of the socialist-oriented parochial school and transferred to a public school. Machray School was much "more authoritative" (qtd. in Binder 83) than Peretz and served students from diverse cultural backgrounds. Students were of Jewish, Polish, Galician, English, and Scottish heritage and the majority of the teachers were of Scottish origin.

Although Waddington had fond memories of her teachers—they "were very nice, [and] I think they had a strong moral sense" (qtd. in Binder 83)—her fellow students were less congenial. During her years at Machray, she regularly heard the racist slur "dirty Jew" and soon learned that "it wasn't good to be Jewish, but ... it was really good to be English" (qtd. in Binder 84).

It was as a grade six student at Machray, however, that Waddington first tried her hand at poetry. She wrote a poem "about spring. I was ten or eleven ... [and] I discovered that I liked writing in rhymes and meter. The teacher praised it, and I wasn't such a great student. It was great to be praised for a poem. She also ... told me that I would have to write more poems. She thought it was very good" (qtd. in Binder 86). Despite their intellectual interests, her parents were less appreciative of their daughter's fledgling achievement. Regardless, Waddington was sufficiently encouraged to write more poems: a ballad entitled "Mermaids" and a narrative poem about "a knight and his lady ... [who] came to a river, the knight and [a] dragon had a battle, the knight was killed. The lady was wearing a mauve dress and she lay down and died of grief. Her dress became the violets" (qtd. in Nickel 185). When her teacher read the poem aloud in class, Waddington's muse was given a boost and she determined to write more poetry.

From the start, writing was both a public and private act for Waddington and her interest in poetry—even as a girl—soon became a source of pride and solace. Although she relished her early success, her poetic skill did not impress her fellow students who favoured scholastic achievement, sports, drama, and fashion over writing and whose disdain for verse was palpable. Whenever she felt uncomfortable, Waddington sought "refuge" in writing and would "go to my room and write a poem" (qtd. in Binder 87). Writing, which soon became a source of pleasure, was Waddington's special talent that she developed and honed as a high school student in Ontario.

In the fall of 1930, her father's business failed due to partnership difficulties and, in the midst of the Great Depression, at age twelve, Waddington moved with her family to Ottawa where she attended Lisgar Collegiate Institute. Neither she nor her family members were content in Ottawa, however, a "provincial town" of 80,000 people (qtd. in Binder 83) with a small, dispersed Jewish community. Waddington relates that there were few non-observant Jews in Ottawa "who had, like my parents, made Yiddish language and culture their home and community" ("Mrs." 1). The Dworkins never fully adjusted to life in Ottawa and soon they began to travel beyond the city's circumscribed borders in search of a larger, more familiar, and certainly more vital Jewish community.

The proximity of Montreal, a comfortable two-hour drive from Ottawa, would prove to be a boon to the aspiring writer. In a third-floor walk-up on Avenue De l'Esplanade, in the heart of Montreal's dense Jewish quarter, lived the Yiddish poet Ida Maza. Having emigrated from Russia as a child, Maza had lived in Montreal most of her life. In Maza's home, which served as a literary salon for Yiddish writers and painters based in Montreal and New York, Waddington began her literary apprenticeship. Under Maza's private coaching and tutelage, Waddington wrote and shared her own poems—at first, "hesitatingly, and with fear"—listened to "poetry being read out loud" by senior writers who often tried "out new ideas for publishing a magazine or a manifesto ... discussed new books and gossiped" ("Mrs." 3, 4), and read the work of Conrad Aiken, Emily Dickinson, Vachel Lindsay, Edna St. Vincent Millay, Sara Teasdale, and Yeats. She also met prominent cultural figures, including the Yiddish poets N. I. Gottlieb, Kadya Molodowsky, Sabsi Perl, J. I. Segal and his sister Esther Segal, Moshe Shaffir, Yudika (Judith Tzik), and the painter Louis Muhlstock.

For several years, Waddington visited Maza in Montreal during school holidays and the Dworkin and Maza families summered together in St. Sauveur, a resort town in the Laurentian mountains north of the city. Maza "radiated a sybilline and mystical quality" ("Mrs." 7) and her love of literature inspired a similar passion in Waddington. She taught her protégée to give "herself entirely and attentively to the poem" ("Mrs." 4) and, although Waddington felt Maza's own verse was too emotional, the degree of Maza's artistic commitment left a profound mark on the young writer. In fact, Waddington's early confidence as a poet was due, in no small part, to the heartfelt support she received from Maza. Moreover, her sustained interest in Jewish literature, confirmed by her own fiction, her scholarly investigation of the work of Canadian poet A.

M. Klein, and her career-long commitment to translating the work of Yiddish writers, can be traced to Maza's formative influence.

Waddington once declared that she was "unambitious" and never considered herself a poet (qtd. in Binder 88), but the record of her early achievement undermines this claim. At the age of ten or eleven, for example, she was awarded a prize for a poem she submitted to a Winnipeg newspaper. At sixteen she won Lisgar Collegiate's annual Arts and Letters Club poetry competition, judged by poet Duncan Campbell Scott, for her poem "The Returner." Poet E. J. Pratt accepted two of her adolescent poems, "Magic" and "The Night Wanderer," for publication in *Canadian Poetry Magazine*. That she wrote regularly and from an early age is evident in the many notebooks and journals she kept during the 1930s. Held in the Miriam Waddington Fonds in Library and Archives Canada, these private books contain early poems and the prose musings of a young woman intent on becoming a writer. Waddington's manuscripts, which fortunately are extant and available for scholarly use, provide ample evidence of an early and sustained writerly commitment and refute the poet's claim that she was a "passive" writer (qtd. in Binder 88) who did not seek public recognition.

Waddington's devaluation of her early vocational commitment may be attributable, in part, to external circumstances that made her feel like an outsider, an "exile" ("Outsider" 42) in her homeland. In elementary school in Winnipeg, she intuited that her "difference, my Jewishness, was seen negatively by Christian children" (37). As a high school student in Ottawa, she was unable to identify with the dominant culture of English Canada, but also admitted to feeling "ambivalent about my parents' immigrant status and my own Jewishness" (40). When she attended the University of Toronto in the 1930s, her sense of separateness was further exacerbated by the absence of Jewish professors—Jews were not hired as teaching faculty until after the Second World War—and the exclusion of Jewish students from Gentile sororities. Later, she would discern that the "unconscious part of me ... was more influenced than I cared to admit by the attitude of the outside world. That world told me in a thousand ways, both subtle and crude, that to be a Jew was a burdensome responsibility" (40). While it may have taken her many years to consciously "bring together and accept my three traditions—the Jewish, the Canadian, and the Russian" (41)—from the late 1930s onward, fiction in particular served as an outlet for Waddington where she could articulate a troubling ambivalence and confusion around issues of identity. Fiction was Waddington's "third world, my own invented one," where she could freely blend the "uniculture" of her Yiddish home and the "multiculture" of English-Canadian life (38).

In her short fiction, written over the course of a long career, Waddington draws on aspects of her own life. Her short stories chart her feelings of isolation and disconnection, and map her personal struggle with her Jewish identity. Taken together, they show her writerly imagination at work, manipulating details of lived experience for narrative effect.

That Waddington chose to open her volume of short stories with "Summer at Lonely Beach" signals her intent to underscore the feelings of alienation and dislocation at the core of her collection. This first-person narrative is recounted by the unnamed, adolescent daughter of Fanya, one of two older women whose friendship is the nucleus of the story. Fanya's friend, Regina Menzies, is Russian, an emancipated intellectual who eschews housework and spends the summer at Manitoba's Lonely Beach reading widely among such works as *A Montessori Mother*, *Mother India*, and Pushkin's poetry. The narrator's curiosity about Menzies is piqued by the woman's decision to rent a cottage on Lonely Beach, apart from the summer colony of Gimli where her own family vacations. She is further intrigued by Menzies's marital status. Although she is known as Miss Menzies, she has a husband and son who live on an Alberta farm. In an effort to understand the considerable influence she wields over her mother, the narrator seeks to peel away the mystery shrouding Menzies.

This story, as much about the constraints of gender roles and the risks adult women take when they challenge social conventions, also charts the adolescent narrator's developing awareness and her final realization that she, too, will confront the difficulties facing her mother and Menzies. As a prescient and intuitive youth whose summer is spent among adult women, the narrator uncovers the truth she seeks—that Menzies is an adulteress who rents a cottage with Dr. Galill, a map-maker who shares her interest in the communist struggle, an "ill-humored" (*Summer* 7) man who is not loath to humiliate the narrator when she questions his political principles—but these revelations finally prove too much for her to bear. By the end of the summer, when she boards the train leaving Gimli for Winnipeg, she has been brought to a fragile understanding of the complexity of human relationships:

> [O]utside the window Miss Menzies and Dr Galill stood waving at us. As the train began to heave and creak out of the station, the smell of lake water and sand came to me through the glass like something alive. We were losing it, losing it!
> 
> Without knowing why, I felt frantic.... But the train was moving and wouldn't stop, and the weak light of the sun hit Miss Menzies' hair and made it glow for the last time, blue-green like peacock feathers. (*Summer* 7)

A profound sense of loss, felt but not fully grasped by the youthful narrator, sets the tone for the volume. Like the three characters of the title story, especially the unnamed female protagonist on the cusp of adulthood, women in subsequent stories often feel circumscribed by gender, seek to challenge prescriptive behavioural norms, and are set adrift by their own devices.

Many of Waddington's protagonists are girls and women whose narrative journeys lead to painful revelations they do not fully comprehend. "A Mixed Marriage," for example, leaves Esther, the first-person narrator, with a disconcerting self-awareness that recalls that of Fanya's daughter in "Summer at Lonely Beach." The second story in the volume, "A Mixed Marriage" tells of Linda and David Solway, a married couple who moves next door to Esther. As Esther befriends Linda, she is afforded a series of glimpses into the state of the Solway's marriage, which shifts dramatically over the course of three years. Another narrator whose third-party perspective ensures a clear, unhampered view, Esther serves as unwilling witness to the demise of a marriage, an experience that jolts her thirteen-year-old sensibilities.

At the start of the narrative, seventeen-year-old Linda Solway is a newlywed with a baby boy. Linda's pregnancy sparked her marriage to David Solway, whose mother disowned him when he chose to marry outside the Jewish faith. Having quit secondary school, David drives a delivery truck for a dry-cleaning company and is struggling to support his young family. "[D]azzled" by her new neighbour, eleven-year-old Esther befriends her "immediately. I admired Linda's baby and she was glad of an audience" (*Summer* 8). An inexperienced Esther is called upon to negotiate parental disapproval—her mother rejects Linda Solway as an inappropriate companion for her daughter—the rocky terrain of the Solway's marriage, and her own uncertain understanding of their relationship. Her role as intermediary emerges as complicated and more difficult than Esther anticipates while she and Linda shop together for groceries, visit the local park, "leaf through love story magazines which I was forbidden to read at home ... [and] decorate ourselves with bangles, brooches and earrings" (9).

The story's multi-layered conflict reflects contemporary values about pre-marital sex and pregnancy, intermarriage, and class difference. Esther's mother, for example, does not want her daughter to visit Linda Solway and her "bastard" (*Summer* 9) baby. She condemns sex outside of marriage, but, more importantly, she fears the influence of intermarriage. That Esther's mother's negative views dominate the narrative—in contrast, her father favours understanding and compassion over judgement and rejection of the Solways—suggests the extent to which women themselves often are complicit in sanctioning female behavioural codes. Six months later, much to Esther's mother's relief, the Solways rent a small house four blocks away "in a poorer district of north Winnipeg" (11). When she visits them in their new home, Esther has matured sufficiently to intuit the class divide that separates the Solways and her family. David has lost his job with the dry-cleaning company and is now working as a department store shipper. Linda and Esther have little to say to one another and Esther admits to feeling "more miserable all the time, yet I did not know how to get up and leave. I wondered wildly why no one had ever taught me to do these things—what did one say, how did one leave?" (12).

The discomfort she feels and the "core of sadness" (*Summer* 12) she recognizes in the Solway home unsettle Esther, but nothing prepares her for a final visit, two years later, when she confronts a drunken, unemployed David who recognizes the "Li'l Joosh girl from next foor" (14). Here, Esther witnesses an unpleasant scene between the Solways and Robert, their successful brother-in-law, who has helped David secure employment in the past. A desperate David, battered by years of failure and remorse—he describes himself as "a no-good drunken bum" (15)—is being coerced by Linda and Robert to sign a paper that would ostensibly finalize his conversion from Judaism.

A traumatized Esther recognizes David's misery and Linda's despair and understands that their present lives are utterly bereft of the hope they once shared. At thirteen, Esther cannot infer the full meaning of the disturbing scene, but she watches with horror as David's will dissipates and Linda's guilt grows visible before her eyes. Assaulted by shame and the loss of family connections, David, in particular, is emblematic of Waddington's characters who lose themselves when they relinquish their cultural identity and inheritance. He also serves as a potent warning for Esther—she innocently declares herself an atheist at an early point in the story—against intermarriage and assimilation. That Esther likely follows David's poor example is implied, however, at the story's close when, as an adult, the faces of the Solways "look out at me from the canvases of [painter] George Rouault. And sometimes, to my horror, I meet them not in paintings but much closer to home" (*Summer* 15). The ending suggests that Esther, like David Solway, has made an undisclosed choice that profoundly affects her life. It is the personal cost associated with such choices, articulated here as a rootless, fragmented sense of self, which is foregrounded in Waddington's stories.

Tamar, the adult narrator of "Far from Snows of Winnipeg," considers several critical choices that have shaped the course of her life. This story, perhaps more than any other in the collection, explicitly probes the experience of what it means to be Jewish, Russian, and Canadian, the "three traditions" ("Outsider" 41) that influenced Waddington herself. Here, three narrative levels enfold and overlap: Tamar's present experience of visiting a friend in hospital where she meets Joseph, an attractive "Jew with the luminous protuberant eyes, the soft hair, the wandering uncontained masculine voice, all held together in a frame which was large-bodied yet delicate and luminous as the whole spirit of the man" (*Summer* 22); her memory of one summer at Workmen's Circle Camp in Ontario where she befriends Niggy, whose "sun-baked innocence, the loneliness that filled him without his ever knowing it, and ... [his need] for nearness to another" (26) held special appeal; and Tamar's ruminations on her current relationship with Hugh, "bright and ginger-colored, a Scotsman, brassy in sunlight. ... The essential thing in Hugh is the mystery I feel in him and my distance from his sources" (23). As she traces the origins and nuances of her connections to these three seminal figures in her life, Tamar's ambivalence and conflicted identity are highlighted.

Tamar's catalytic meeting with Joseph spurs her thoughts about Judaism. Despite his frailness (the result of a rheumatic heart) and dilettantism, Tamar finds Joseph charming, even erotically appealing, but does not encourage his advances. She consciously admits to an "inability to love in another Jew whatever it is we call manhood." She believes that Jews are too close for love: "Sometimes I have even thought we Jews are all the same sex. I could never love a Jew for I know him far too well in his ancient impersonal lineaments, in that very core which in love ought to remain mysterious" (*Summer* 22). By the time Tamar meets Joseph, she has given serious thought to the religious, cultural, and emotional ties that, in her view, bind all Jews. Moreover, since she believes a romantic union with Joseph would unveil the essential "weakness" (24) that drives Jews to seek out one another, she consciously avoids such a liaison.

She has not always been cognizant, however, of the deep-rooted anxiety elicited by Joseph's demeanour. At summer camp with fellow outsider Niggy (who lacks the religious education of the other campers), for example, when a Ukrainian handyman "emptied a bucket of water on the floor and roared out a string of curses in Russian, some of which I had heard in my childhood days in the alleys of North Winnipeg" (*Summer* 28), Tamar's involuntary response is to sob uncontrollably and feel shame and humiliation. For the eighteen-year-old Tamar, her Russian background, Jewish faith, and Canadian upbringing, brought into relief in the setting of socialist summer camp, do not form a comfortable, coherent identity. Her youthful response to visceral confusion—in the wake of "paroxysms" (28) of tears—is to compartmentalize her heightened feelings and to seek an intellectual understanding of what it means to be Jewish.

Hugh, her current lover whose Scottish background evokes "warrior[s], hiding out in the moors, burning with rebellion," embodies the strength necessary to "shelter" Tamar and "hide" (*Summer* 23, 24) her sense of weakness. That she can "worship [him as] a mystery" (22-23) suggests that Hugh's difference holds immense appeal for a Jewish woman who vacillates between the conflicting desire to embrace her cultural inheritance or abandon her heritage. As she admits,

> I do all the things other Jews do. I listen to recordings of Israeli songs. I buy books of Yiddish poems privately printed if I am importuned enough by the author, and occasionally, when warm with whiskey, I sing Jewish songs to old gypsy melodies. Yet all the time I'm baffled by the inconsolable strangeness of this transplanted landscape halfway between Europe and North America. (*Summer* 28-29)

Tamar's dilemma is characteristic of Waddington's female protagonists who feel at odds with themselves, their cultural legacy, and their Canadian home. She is a conflicted individual who seeks comfort in the external, superficial signs of Judaism—songs and poems—but will not commit to her faith. Her sense of cultural dislocation is even greater in the context of Canada, the "transplanted landscape" of her exile. As a mature adult, Tamar knows "the ground under us has shifted," but she remains confused, "on the brink of something new" where memory is "suspended and hovering" (*Summer* 30, 29). Alienated from her culture and country, her memory detached from time and place, hers is a rootless malaise that pervades the volume.

For Mrs. Land, the social worker who narrates "The Last Rehearsal," the ground shifts perceptibly during a brief encounter with an elderly Jewish couple. To access their cramped and shabby flat, Mrs. Land must climb a "rickety flight of stairs ... trundle over the plank which is laid across" a gravel path, make her "way between two clotheslines with their flannelette nightgowns and suits of union underwear blowing in the wind," and pass "an ancient chicken coop ... garbage and a broken enameled pot" (*Summer* 34). The obstacles that physically hinder her entry to the circumscribed world of Pearl and her husband mirror the psychological hurdle Mrs. Land confronts as she offers medical assistance that will reverse Pearl's encroaching blindness from cataracts. The couple's adamant refusal of the care she proffers forces Mrs. Land to accept the irreconcilable clash of cultural differences.

Denied a "blind pension" (*Summer* 37) because Pearl refuses to undergo a cataract operation, she and her husband are obliged to live on his meagre pensioner's income. At first, the couple's fear of doctors and hospitalization appears irrational to Mrs. Land whose faith in the medical profession is shaped by her Canadian experience. Soon, however, she gleans the source of their apprehension. Long ago in Russia, the couple sought medical help for their fourteen-year-old daughter who contracted scarlet fever. When Pearl brought the girl to the hospital, she encountered a doctor who "'was a terrible anti-Semite. I just turned my back a minute, not more, and he gave her the last rehearsal [i.e., he killed her].'" As Pearl's husband confirms, "'they watch for us, those young doctors. They see a Jewish face in the clinic, and they right away plan to poison it, kill it off'" (36). The couple's profound mistrust of doctors, influenced by their formative experience of racism in Russia, is transferred to Canada. While Mrs. Land discerns the vast cultural differences that separate Russia and Canada, the couple is unable to make the same distinctions. Hence, they are suspicious of all doctors and dentists and believe irrationally that a thief has secured entry to their flat, stolen the goose down from their quilts, and replaced it with chicken feathers.

As a fellow Jew, Mrs. Land is welcomed as a "real guest" (*Summer* 37) by the couple who believe she understands the reasoning behind their refusal of a necessary operation. Although she must concede defeat and is unable to provide the desired pension, Mrs. Land herself is brought to new awareness. As she steps out into "the clear cold air" (37), she is startled when six starlings fly up in her face. For the moment, her vision is altered. She does not see herself as a young professional who has lived a life of sheltered ease in Canada. Instead, almost blinded by the birds, she is unnerved, forced to recognize the cultural ties that unite her and the aged couple. Moreover, she begins to think "about being old" (37) and, the ending implies, how her own youthful ideas will bear on her elderly self. The psychological chasm that separates the social worker and her clients at the start of the narrative is bridged by their shared cultural inheritance as Jews, which serves finally as the basis for connection and potential renewal for Mrs. Land.

Vanessa, the protagonist of "The Honeymoon House," also experiences a measure of renewal, but only after she relives painful memories of a former connection with Carl Agricola, a repressed homosexual. The story centres on two relationships: Vanessa's three-and-a-half-year affair with Carl and her current marriage to "a prosperous middle-aged accountant" with whom she shares "a house with leaded windows and a double garage in Toronto's Forest Hill" (*Summer* 50), an affluent Jewish neighbourhood. Every six months, when he feels depressed, Carl telephones Vanessa who has lingering feelings for him and buoys his mood. The narrative hinges on one such telephone call, but, in this instance, Vanessa is no longer willing to succour Carl. Instead, she breaks her ties with her former lover and announces, "'I'm married now, so there's not much point in telephoning me any more'" (52). Vanessa's decisiveness belies her emotional wounds and powerful memories of her romance with Carl.

Vanessa's deep love for Carl was transformative. When she and Carl made love, "they became one shadow and one darkness"; often, she was transported to the past of her Jewish childhood in the Ukraine, with its whitewashed prairie houses, gardens of forget-me-nots and zinnias, "the hot dusty smell of chokecherries by the river" (*Summer* 53). Carl helped assuage the sense of personal loss Vanessa had internalized since leaving the Ukraine; his presence tempered her solitary suffering and his conversation was healing. After years, however, "mending and remending the broken web in the darkness" (53), when Carl could not return her love, Vanessa ended their relationship.

Vanessa's subsequent marriage surprised everyone who had known her and Carl. At first, the rich, imaginative world that Vanessa inhabits with Carl contrasts with the home she shares with her accountant husband. An impressive house, built as a wedding gift for the daughter of "a famous Hollywood actor," it shelters Vanessa in her grief. Once she severs her connection with Carl, however, the house and the life it contains—Vanessa, her two children, her husband—become "more and more golden," awash with the sun that "flowed in through the open doors." A bird sings "in the shrubbery at the end of the garden," the sun shines on the "gold-colored carpets" and the "gold moldings of new picture frames." As Vanessa moves fully into the present to embrace a world of her own choosing in a beautiful home on an urban Canadian street, Carl's links to her past in the Ukraine and inability to offer her love are rendered sterile. Here, renewal is possible when the past is abandoned in favour of the present. But Vanessa's reprieve is qualified, for, she concedes, "her grief had ripened like wheat. Her heart was full and heavy with it. But ... who in this wide world would ever reap it now?" (*Summer* 54). The variegated contours of grief—lament for a cultural inheritance, a childhood, a love lost—are shrouded by the sunlight that momentarily illuminates her home, but linger still on the edges of Vanessa's life. The open question with which the story ends, although celebratory in tone, invokes an abiding melancholy that permeates Vanessa's adult experience as a Jewish woman residing in Canada.

Grief and fear also drive thirty-eight-year-old Mignon Carmichael, the protagonist of "A Silence All Too Long," to seek out love with a new partner. Mignon's twenty-year marriage to Leo Carmichael has ended in scandal. The couple lived in Montreal with their two sons and enjoyed a suburban life of "comfort and reassurance" (*Summer* 64). When Leo decides, however, to leave Mignon to marry a "rich forty-five-year old widow who was ... enamored of him," she packs her belongings and moves with her sons to Toronto. Mignon has difficulty adjusting to her new life as a divorcée and cannot forget Leo's cruel, parting words: "'you know nothing about sex, nothing!'" Moreover, that the Carmichaels, like Linda and David Solway, are a mixed couple—Mignon is Jewish and Leo is "Maritime Scots" (65)—may account, in part, for the demise of their marriage. Two years after divorcing Leo, when Mignon finally decides to date another man, she chooses fellow painter Joseph Rieder, an Islamic Studies professor of Arab descent. Divorced himself, Joseph, who is Mignon's age and shares her artistic interests, facilitates her emotional and spiritual recovery, but only after his amorous advances force her to confront her own ambivalent sexual feelings and accept her identity as a newly single Jewish woman.

Mignon's partners—men of Scottish and Arab heritage, respectively—and the conflict that ensues with each, compel her to reflect on her own cultural background. Although she identifies herself as "one generation removed from the wheat fields of the Ukraine" and avoids indulging her "Russian soul in self pity" or her "Hebraic one in prophecies of doom"—"It's written all over you that you're Russian from the cheekbones down, and all Jew from the eyes up. That's your inheritance, so put up with it!" (*Summer* 68)—she is fully assimilated into Canadian society. Through marriage to a Gentile, residency in cosmopolitan Montreal where everyone "appeared to be alike, of one great mixed culture, hot, vulgar, and beautiful" (67), and her profession—three of her paintings hang in Canada's National Gallery—she has integrated into the larger society.

When she leaves Montreal, however, Mignon's equilibrium is disturbed. No longer a wife of twenty years, she is dating a man she does not know well. Toronto is an alien, windy city, "old, too, red brick and intersecting streetcar tracks, shabby, bleak and Upper Canada" (*Summer* 64). She soon regrets her decision to lodge temporarily with her aged aunt who is ill-tempered, morose, and impatient with her sons. Moreover, her work "for a large commercial art firm ... [is] new, difficult to master, and uninteresting" and her colleagues are "cool Protestants, restrained and washed-out looking" (67). Although her situation improves when she rents an apartment of her own in the leafy neighbourhood of Rosedale and sends her sons to boarding school over the winter, Mignon feels uneasy in Toronto.

Her sense of dislocation is exacerbated by her February encounter with Joseph in his apartment. Although they had met several times and Mignon "felt attracted by his strong and sensual good looks ... the healthy ruddiness which shines magnetically from red-haired men" (*Summer* 68), she rebuffs his sexual advances, turns cold, and, as his caresses intensify, begins to sob uncontrollably, like Tamar in "Far from Snows of Winnipeg." Her grief "rise[s] like waves, breaking her open with a force and misery that she had never dreamed could be hidden in a human soul, much less her own" (*Summer* 71). Overcome by her own extreme response to Joseph's sexual overture, Mignon loses composure.

The turbulent release of sorrow, at first frightening, proves restorative, however. Newly aware that "I really don't know much about sex. Nor about myself either," Mignon feels "light with relief" (*Summer* 71) and free to initiate a frank discussion with Joseph. As they move toward reconciliation—Joseph admits to feeling hurt by her rejection and Mignon to self-doubt—the couple plans a June meeting when the catalpa tree in Joseph's yard will blossom. The brevity of their emotional exchange belies a profound shift in Mignon who now senses that Toronto offers an opportunity to assemble "the puzzling shapes and untried colors of her own broken life" (73). The beckoning light of Joseph's kitchen at the close of the narrative recalls the soothing sunlight that bathes Vanessa's home at the conclusion of "The Honeymoon House." That Mignon is offered a newly lighted path, away from the pain of the past in Montreal toward a hopeful, uncharted future in Toronto, affirms the malleable strength of her identification as a Jew and a Canadian.

Hannah Sayers, the protagonist of "Breaking Bread in Jerusalem," appears to be a middle-aged version of Mignon Carmichael. Hannah is a forty-five-year-old childless divorcée who seeks to reclaim her Jewish heritage by traveling to Israel in search of "a new direction for her life" (*Summer* 74). Unlike Mignon, who carefully plans her move from Montreal to Toronto, Hannah sells her weaving studio, closes her Toronto apartment, and flies to Tel Aviv without a predetermined destination. She settles in Jerusalem where she rents an apartment, but soon travels to the southern city of Eilat for a five-day holiday where a chance meeting influences her perception of the country and herself. Yacob, an Egyptian Jew who moved to Israel following his mother's death, proclaims, "you will see for yourself, everyone who comes here, serves this country's purpose" (77), a prophecy that impresses Hannah and colours her stay in Eilat. Unlike Mignon, however, whose personal transformation is facilitated by Joseph, Hannah's quest for self-discovery is undertaken alone.

Hannah's search "for something, she didn't know what" takes her to The Castle, a small island near Eilat. There, by the "hypnotic" seashore, she revisits the past through memory to uncover "a part of herself which she had long ago consigned to darkness" (*Summer* 77, 82, 80). She reconsiders her decision to remain single after her two-year marriage to Max had ended when she discovered he was having an affair. That Max leaves her for a Gentile woman causes Hannah to speculate:

> A lot of Jewish men were like Max; they didn't like Jewish women. Incest taboo or something else? Jewish women were too serious, always expected marriage, nagged, reminded them of their mothers. Or ... in a more subtle way it was their fathers they were really running away from, rebelling against. Or then again maybe they were just paying back old debts. Hadn't Abraham sent Hagar and Hagar's child away? His sons would therefore right old wrongs and marry her daughters. (82)

Unlike Mignon, Hannah yearns to reconnect with her Jewish heritage and believes a romantic partnership with a fellow Jew is appropriate.

When she falls asleep on the beach, Hannah's memories collide in dreams that leave her feeling "light and happy" (*Summer* 84). She addresses her grandfather in Yiddish, revisits the streets and districts of London, England, returns to her parents' comfortable home in Winnipeg with its Russian samovar and life-size portrait of the Yiddish writer I. L. Peretz, and listens to a Yiddish folk song often sung by her grandmother. She also endures a loneliness that "wraps her round like a cape, laps her round like a sea, until she becomes a boat herself, anchored close to shore, rocking, gently rocking," and realizes "it's kisses you've been wanting all this time. Kisses" (83, 84).

Hannah's cultural identity is restored and redefined on Israeli soil. She develops an attachment to the country, its history, geography, and people, which connects with the various cultures—Yiddish,

Russian, British, Canadian—that have shaped her particular experience of the world. Further, as she increasingly feels at home in Israel, she overcomes her fear of strangers. On The Castle, for example, she shares a thermos of coffee with a local Arab watchman who once appeared threatening. By communing with the land and its people—the Jewish Yacob and the Arab watchman—she embraces the richness of the past and the potential of the present, embodied in the "radiant" city of Jerusalem whose "light from its towers would warm her through all the winters she had ever lived or ever would" (*Summer* 84).

That her experience of Israel affords Hannah an unprecedented sense of cultural equilibrium and inner peace affirms the physical and spiritual impact of the country on her Jewish sensibility. The narrative suggests that Israel welcomes all diasporic Jews and makes possible the reclaiming of one's roots. Having been cleansed and renewed, Hannah is rewarded with a redemptive vision of the future that is bathed in light and warmth. Indeed, more so than any of Waddington's female protagonists, Hannah's quest ends positively, with the contours of her life softened and reshaped. The story celebrates Israel as an ideal, a place where Jewish identity can be forged anew. Its unique narrative harmony, coming toward the close of the volume, resonates with readers as emblematic of Waddington's incontestable valuing of cultural roots and the significant influence they bear on female identity.

Waddington's writerly probing of identity began early. In a journal entry, dated 22 October 1943, the aspiring author notes:

> this problem of identity ... first I sink into the entity of me—Miriam. Then Miriam is absorbed & sunk & drowned in the great beard of Jew. Then, outside that circle, or interwoven, is the area of system. I identify with a communist system.... Then there's the world. Physical world of streets, sun, people, jazz. In all of these are me. And so easily am I lost in them. Where's the problem of identity?
>
> Of course, when I was a lad [sic] I often stopped & thought to myself. "What if this is a play, & I'm acting on a stage and someone's watching. Suppose I wake up and find I'm not me at all."

> This feeling always amazed me, gave me a feeling of being a stranger in the world. I suppose in a small way it was my groping for identity. (Notebook)

In her short stories, Waddington investigates aspects of identity enumerated in this seminal articulation of her self in the world: Miriam as woman, Jew, and Socialist; as social being stimulated by urban life and enthralled by nature; admirer of beauty, art, and artifice; as outsider and exile. Hers is a fragmented sense of self.

Waddington's female characters share their author's experience of fragmentation and the sense of "being a stranger in the world" characterizes each of their stories. The first-person narrator of the final story, "I'm Lonesome for Harrisburg," describes, for example, her "emotional map": located at the centre is grief, surrounded by sorrow, pain, and loneliness (*Summer* 86), emotions that govern the collection.[1] Although each protagonist struggles to reconcile the emotional and spiritual conflict she feels as a woman, a Jew, and a Canadian, she betrays a persistent, uncanny detachment that remains at the heart of *Summer at Lonely Beach*. With the unique exception of Hannah Sayers, Waddington's female characters are estranged from religious, cultural, and national roots and their respective narratives move outward, eschewing resolution in favour of openness.

Irresolution ought not to be read as failure on the author's part to come to terms with a multifaceted cultural identity, however. For Waddington understands "[c]ulture, Jewish culture … [as] a much wider and more inclusive matter." More specifically, she invokes the spectres of Yiddish writers as her talismans: "If I had to sum up what being a secular Jew means to me, I would have to say that it means having Peretz on the dining-room wall, Mendele Mocher Sforim and the poets [Halper] Leyvick and [Itzik] Manger looking over my shoulder as I write, and—to keep things alive and moving—Sholom Aleichem in my heart" ("Outsider" 41). Waddington's reverence for writing is twofold: writing serves as a vehicle for cultural reconciliation—however fleeting, however brief—and an incomparable means of exploring the distinctive and complex identity of Jewish Canadian women.

## Notes

[1]Of the six remaining stories in *Summer at Lonely Beach and Other Stories,* "The Halloween Party," "A Place of Witches," and "Waldemar" explore the experiences of male protagonists, and "Day in the Sun," "Farewells at Four O'Clock," and "The Water Cooler" reflect the author's professional experience as a social worker. Since they lie outside the scope of this essay, I have refrained from discussing them here.

## Works Cited

Binder, Wolfgang. "An Interview with Miriam Waddington." *Commonwealth Essays and Studies* 11.2 (1989): 83-84.

Moritz, Albert. "Profile: From a Far Star." *Books in Canada* May 1982: 5-8.

Nickel, Barbara. "Following the Breath into Form." *Where the Words Come From: Canadian Poets in Conversation.* Ed. Tim Bowling. Roberts Creek, BC: Nightwood Editions, 2002. 184-95.

Waddington, Miriam. "Mrs. Maza's Salon." *Apartment Seven: Essays Selected and New.* By M. Waddington. Studies in Canadian Literature. Don Mills, ON: Oxford University Press, 1989. 1-8.

Waddington, Miriam. Notebook. Miriam Waddington Fonds. R4777-0-2-E. Library and Archives Canada, Ottawa.

Waddington, Miriam. "Outsider: Growing Up in Canada." *Apartment Seven: Essays Selected and New.* By M. Waddington. Studies in Canadian Literature. Don Mills, ON: Oxford University Press, 1989. 36-44.

Waddington, Miriam. *Summer at Lonely Beach and Other Stories.* Oakville, ON: Mosaic Press/Valley Editions, 1982.

# 2.
# "Ambiguity and Paradox"

## A Conversation with Helen Weinzweig

Helen Weinzweig is the author of two novels, *Passing Ceremony* (1973), *Basic Black with Pearls* (1980), and a collection of short stories, *A View from the Roof* (1989). At the age of nine, she emigrated from Poland to Canada, where her formal education began. An only child, Weinzweig was raised by her divorced mother. She did not know her father until she was an adult. Weinzweig's career as a writer began when she was forty-five. The wife of composer, John Weinzweig, Helen immersed herself in her husband's work and learned about structure and technique from his development of twelve-tone music. Her narratives are dark, spare, and her characters are set adrift by the circumstances of their lives. Weinzweig's fragmented, discontinuous texts propel her readers toward a heightened awareness of the chaos of contemporary life. Currently, she is working on a third novel, which she describes here as "statement, without adjectives and adverbs." In May 1998, I met with Helen Weinzweig at her Toronto home where we spoke for three hours.

RP: *Helen, how did you come to write at the age of forty-five?*

HW: I had twenty different jobs from the time I went to work at seventeen. I was trying to improve myself by going from job to job, working part-time and full-time. Well, I was forty-five, my two sons were on their own, my husband got a job at the University of Toronto, and suddenly I didn't need to work anymore. I fell apart because the struggle for economic survival was over.

I went to a woman psychiatrist because I didn't know what to do with my life. In the 1930s and '40s women were expected to play out their roles as wives and mothers. But on my first visit—out of arrogance, despair, and fear—I announced, "I don't want to adjust!" She responded, "Yours is a simple problem of integration." I was a little miffed because I didn't think there was anything simple about my existence. Fortunately, she wasn't interested in prolonged analysis. One of my problems was that, despite a passion for books, I could no longer read: the printed word did not impinge. She suggested I find my own words. But *I* couldn't write. Then, on an empty white sheet in the typewriter, I started to free associate and the first line I wrote was, "Your body cares not a whit for your mind." I almost started to cry.

I then spent two years writing a short story that I sent out and it got published. Two years later I sent out another story and it got published. I panicked. Did publication mean I could write? Could I be a writer? I continued with another story.

RP: *What did you read as a young woman?*

HW: I was the only one I knew who hadn't read [Louisa May Alcott's] *Little Women*. I read the *Boys' Own Annual*. I did not like women's fiction. I didn't like the women I knew. That wasn't their fault, but I didn't want their lives. I did not see myself as a woman until I started writing.

There is a picture of me aboard ship to Europe in 1932. For the Captain's Ball, a costumed event, I borrowed a pair of trousers from a young chap I knew. As half man-half woman, I dressed in one trouser leg and half a skirt. I drew a moustache above half my lips and applied lipstick to the other half. It kills me to look at this picture of me at seventeen. What is that? My husband claims that I confuse people. He says people don't know what to expect from me. What does he mean? But a funny thing happened on my way to becoming a writer. I "integrated" to such an extent that I developed hips and breasts. I'm not kidding; in places, I am twice the size I used to be.

RP: *Who directed your reading?*

HW: I arrived here when I was nine and I had never been to school. I didn't know how to read and write. In Poland, when I was six, I went to school for one day, a policeman brought me home, and then I wouldn't go back. When I was in my thirties, my mother explained that she had to obtain shoes and clothes for me to go to school, that she sent me to school when it had been underway for weeks. In class, the kids sat down and immediately opened their books. But I didn't have a book, so I took one from someone's desk. When I was leaving school with the book, someone called the police to say I had stolen a book. I never returned because I felt so ashamed to have been arrested.

When we came to Canada, we lived with my aunt and uncle who ran a restaurant at Spadina and Dundas [in Toronto]. My two cousins made fun of me because I couldn't speak English. At ten, I had to learn how to read, write, and speak English quickly. At fifteen, I was first in my class in high school.

My mother worked and she didn't get along with anybody. My mother and my aunt quarrelled, my uncle was busy womanizing and running a restaurant, and so I had nowhere to go after school. Then I discovered Boys and Girls House [now Lillian H. Smith branch, Toronto Public Library] where I was adopted by a librarian, Miss Bush. She gave me hot chocolate and read to me. She was the first and only person who cared about me and we communicated through books.

The first book I ever read was [J. M. Barrie's] *Peter Pan*. I lived at Spadina and Dundas and I used to look for the statue of Peter Pan on Kensington Avenue. I thought I was in England.

RP: *Do you think your work reflects your experience as a woman?*

HW: I have a lot of trouble with that. Everything I had read had been written by men and from the male point of view. I was terrified when I tried to put words on paper. "What can I say that is mine? Who needs another book? What is mine that is different from the things I have read? Nothing, nothing is mine. Everything I know has come from books or necessity. What have I got to say?" It took about ten years for me to learn to use first person. I wrote everything in third person. Third person was easy because "I" didn't exist. The first person had to be found: who was the first person, who was the "I"?

I have modified a lot of my vocabulary. For example, a phrase I no longer use is "playing a role." It's in the language, it's acceptable, yet I resent it. I have never played a role in my life, but I was using "my role as mother," "my role as teacher," etc. Suddenly I realized that the phrase is acceptable for women *only* because it adds to their sense of fragmentation. So I've begun to watch my vocabulary and to question the idea that I am a different woman as a mother and as a writer. I decided that what may be considered "normal" was not normal for me.

RP: *I am struck by your faceless female characters. Do you see them as faceless?*

HW: Someone once said that all my women are victims. My response was, "Yes, but they prevail." Because of my own limited background, I cannot seem to enter into the life of the well-adjusted and apparently successful woman who has an ability to handle her crises directly. This may be because I wish to talk about events in my personal life. In fiction I seem to regress to a period in my own life when I had no sense of identity.

RP: *Your work has been described as unsettling, Helen.*

HW: I'm always surprised by that because in the process of writing this unsettling material, I settled something in myself. I guess what was a catharsis for me becomes a difficulty for the reader.

Everything I have written has been a discovery for me. Unwittingly, I found a source in myself that I wanted to tap. It was the not-knowing that propelled my writing, not knowing what was going on, not having any judgement. For me, fiction is the truth of the unconscious, if it's done properly.

RP: *Do you see a connection between your fiction and your husband's music?*

HW: Two scholars at Lakehead University [S. R. MacGillivray and Noreen Ivancic] say that my husband's twelve-tone technique has shaped my writing.

RP: *What do you think? You have said yourself that you lived John's career.*

HW: Yes, I did. Vicariously I lived out the trials and agonies of

John's career. My energy, creativity, and thought went into John. There wasn't a thought in the world that I could do anything on my own, not a thought. I flattered John into marrying me. I was his muse; I provided titles for his work; I stayed up with him until all hours to talk about his music. But when I got pregnant with Paul the emphasis shifted away from John and I don't think he ever got over it.

I went to night school when Paul was a baby to get my senior matriculation and thought maybe I'd go to school again. The history teacher met me at the door one evening and said, "Please, Mrs. Weinzweig, not tonight." I said, "I'm sorry." I would disrupt the class by asking questions on history, "but, but sir." And so I realized I couldn't go back. I could no longer just sit there and "repeat after me." So, I didn't go back to school, I didn't get my senior matriculation, and I didn't go to university.

When my sons were babies, I trained in nursery school work. I organized the first co-operative nursery school on our street, which began in the basement of my house. And I started to think, well, I can learn child psychology and do nursery school work. But I couldn't continue because it was very hard for my sons to have other children come into their house and claim their mother's attention.

RP: *So, Helen, are you saying that there is a connection between your own and John's work?*

HW: Yes. For twelve years we lived in a small house and the piano was alongside the kitchen wall. I was in the kitchen a good deal of the time when I wasn't doing nursery school work or whatever. My place was preparing meals, cleaning up, and all the rest of it. John was at the piano most of the time because he always worked at home.

Due to circumstances beyond my control, I have always been alert to my environment, and unconsciously I was alert to the environment of competent musical composition. So when I heard John working out an idea, often I would go in and say, "Not yet, not yet. A little more, a little more." I can't read music but something in me began to feel the process. I could sense the structure of a composition, even when it wasn't in the traditional three parts. I could sense

37

where it was going and feel the inevitability of a piece.

I will work on a paragraph for as long as a month or rewrite one page twenty times until it has that same inevitability. So that is where possibly I absorbed structure. I hate to admit it because part of me is still a little bit uneasy with thirty years of the vicarious life that women of my generation lived. The careers of men were often the work of their wives. I can't blame myself but there is a vestige of regret.

RP: *How did you react to your first publication?*

HW: I didn't know that the *Canadian Forum* had accepted my first story, "Surprise!" [in 1968]. Everybody sent his or her first story to the *Canadian Forum*. I was walking along the street, the *Forum* was displayed in a wire rack outside a bookstore, and my name leapt out at me from the cover. Seeing my name in print on the cover of the *Canadian Forum* was a thrilling moment.

I then went to New York to take a writing course. I took with me an unpublished short story and I discovered—I was forty-eight years old at the time—that the young students were indignant that there were old people in the course with them. They were graduate students in their early to mid-twenties and they didn't like the presence of oldies.

RP: *What inspired your first novel,* **Passing Ceremony***?*

HW: My husband had a performance in Saskatoon, I think it was, where we visited our host's friend, Eli Bornstein, a painter. He had a painting on his wall. Within the frame were blocks of wood painted white, in various geometric shapes and sizes. While the men were talking I was staring and it hit me that if I had material that was geometrical and enclosed it in a frame, I could do in a novel what he had done on canvas. The random shapes and their random placement were unified by the frame. And the other unity was geometry.

In *Passing Ceremony*, I found the frame in an experience I had at a friend's wedding and everything took place within that frame. But I couldn't maintain the unity entirely; I was not experienced enough. Everything should have occurred within the frame of the wedding but I had the characters driving around Toronto, going to High Park. I gave up. I couldn't find any more material within the frame. I can now, but I gave up then. I saw unity on Eli Bornstein's wall and I repeated it in *Passing Ceremony*. It took six years to write.

I knew I had done a modern thing. No continuity, explanations, or flashbacks, and some of the characters aren't named. There was only one publisher in Canada I knew about that might be interested and that was House of Anansi Press. I took it down by streetcar—at that time they were on Jarvis Street [in Toronto]—and left the manuscript on the receptionist's desk. I got a call that they were interested if I would make some changes. Their editor was—memory, there we go again, senility—Jim Polk. At the time, I wondered why Anansi grabbed it. But I soon realized that everyone's marriage at the Press was breaking up and I bring in *Passing Ceremony* [loud laughter]. Later, when *Basic Black with Pearls* was published, the *New Yorker* commented that my timing was perfect.

Jim Polk said that I had to rewrite, that some things in the novel didn't fit. I picked up the manuscript and the whole thing fell out of my hands onto the floor. As the two of us were gathering the typewritten pages, I said, "This is my first book and I don't know about rewriting. I don't know about what fits and what doesn't fit." So he took a red pen and went through the pages.

When I got home, I read his comments about my inconsistent style and I finally understood. It's *style*! I had absorbed so many literary styles and I had put them all into the book. That's how I learned to edit my work and when I handed the novel back to Jim, he said "It's perfect, but you may be interested to know that Peggy [Atwood] read both versions and she thinks that I was too hard on you, that it's now too spare." There is no word in there that doesn't fit.

RP: *Tell me about the writing of* **Basic Black with Pearls**.

HW: *Basic Black* reflects my desire to belong to the bourgeois, nuclear family. The inherent conflict was to want it and to despise it. I did not write the novel to satisfy readers' expectations.

For public readings, I often used the "cash register" scene in *Basic Black* because I liked it and thought I did well with it. In one of those readings, I froze. I looked out at the audience who were waiting for the next sentence and finally I said, "I can't read this." I had been reading it for about three years. I looked down at one of my friends sitting in the front row and asked her to finish reading for me. She came up to the podium and I took her place in the audience.

When I got home that night, I realized that what I thought I had invented had actually taken place. Unbeknownst to me, I was using unconscious material that did not surface until I had read it—I don't know how many times—as if it were an invention. That evening, in the middle of the reading, my conscious and unconscious merged. When my unconscious entered my memory the whole scene exploded for me. I just about broke down because that was one of my early traumas. Each noon, my aunt would give my two cousins money for candy. But she would slam the cash register shut in my face because I was not entitled to candy. Fortunately, many human traumas remain buried.

Due to circumstances beyond my control, I could not participate in life around me until I was an adult. But I absorbed a lot of what I saw, so many of my characters are voyeurs, like Shirley in *Basic Black*.

RP: *How do you know whether material is appropriate for a short story or a novel?*

HW: I didn't attempt a novel until I had some skill at putting words on paper. There are writers who reserve good material for a novel, but I let the punch line of a story determine its form.

RP: *You've also written drama, Helen.*

HW: The short story, "My Mother's Luck," was adapted for the stage. I also wrote a play about my father, "A Classical Education," which was produced when I was playwright-in-residence at Tarragon Theatre [in Toronto].

In "My Mother's Luck," I struggled to write about my mother's experiences and to give her the voice of a Jewish immigrant. I was proud that the English in the monologue was a transliteration of Yiddish. I was not going to have her speak a "proper" English since she would have spoken in Yiddish if she were actually telling me the story.

I was pleased that I could create a dramatic effect without using dramatic language. The dramatic effect is that the daughter never speaks. The story succeeds entirely because of its *style* and the *two* characters, only one of whom speaks. When it was produced, I walked out of the theatre in tears—my identification with the silent girl was so complete—and my two sons were visibly shaken.

I then got a scholarship to take a playwright's course at Banff [Centre, Alberta]. I wanted to work on the play about my father, a companion piece to "My Mother's Luck." But I couldn't write about my father. At seventeen, I spent three months in an apartment in Italy with my father but now I can't remember his face. He refused to be written about and I put the play away. Some stories can't be written because they're true.

RP: *Would you describe the novel you are working on now?*

HW: The novel that I have been working on for more than ten years presents a problem. I am trying to make simple "reality" fresh and interesting. Instead of starting with what I don't know and working toward discovery, I'm doing the opposite. Now discovery is in the ordinary, everyday world. The challenge is to write about the ordinary and move the reader at the same time.

The more experimental I am, the more control I need. The most important element in experiment is style and in this novel I control style as statement, without adjectives and adverbs. I eschew interior monologue that I use in my earlier work. I want to express thought so the reader responds emotionally, not the character.

Recently, I realized what I set out to do ten years ago. I am really into chaos theory. Physics has shown that there is no order in nature, the universe, or life itself. But strangely, strangely there is a pattern if you can find it. About a year or so ago, I discovered a pattern in the novel's chaotic structure. In my chaotic way of writing, connections are made in the reader's head. In my view, linear thought and therefore linear writing are unnatural to humans.

Having been brought up under traumatic conditions in a *shtetl*, I write the way I heard speech used. No two sentences were consecutive: "*Oy*. What's happening? What should I do? Listen, did you know the woman who lives downstairs, her husband has left her? So, what's going to happen to the children? Oh, my son is learning the Talmud. What's your son doing?" And so it went. I grew up perfectly comfortable with such melodrama, but I want to write melodrama in a postmodern way.

The protagonist in this novel can't remember his childhood and into the text I throw a story, "The Sea at Bar." This story has a linear plot that has nothing to do with the novel but I include it as a likely reason for his amnesia.

I want to write in a manner that avoids what Gertrude Stein called "mere statement." Since I appreciate ambiguity and paradox, I say things on paper that may startle the reader but do not startle me. Now I discard material that does not startle me. I am aiming for sincerity, without props, *shtick*, or nonsense.

For me, process is all. And I've been lucky; I've never had a rejection slip. But I've had to choose between being a writer and, as I say, a "liver." Dostoevsky once said, "Everyday I have to choose whether to live or write." It took me a long time to become a contented writer and I'm not giving that up.

## Selected Bibliography

### Novels

*Passing Ceremony*. Toronto: House of Anansi Press, 1973.
*Basic Black with Pearls*. Toronto: House of Anansi Press, 1980.

### Short Stories

*A View from the Roof*. Fredericton: Goose Lane Editions, 1989.
"The Sea at Bar." *Parchment: Contemporary Canadian Jewish Writing* 2 (1993-94): 11-18.

### Plays

*A Classical Education*. Alberta Theatre Productions, n.d.
*My Mother's Luck*. Prod. Rina Fraticelli, with Pol Pelletier. Factory Theatre Lab, Toronto, May 1983.
*A View from the Roof*. Adapted by Dave Carley. Tarragon Theatre, Toronto, June 1996.

## Non-fiction

"Field Guide to the Care and Feeding of Composers." *Canadian Composer* 17 (April 1967): 8, 44.

"Personal Note." *Canada Writes! The Members' Book of the Writers' Union of Canada*. Ed. K. A. Hamilton. Toronto: Writers' Union of Canada, 1977. 362-63.

"So What Is Real?" *Quarry* 34.2 (Spring 1985): 72-77.

"The Interrupted Sex." *Language in Her Eye: Views on Writing and Gender by Canadian Women Writing in English*. Eds. Libby Scheier, Sarah Sheard, and Eleanor Wachtel. Toronto: Coach House Press, 1990. 297-301.

## Interviews

Bauer, Nancy. "Nancy Bauer Interviews Helen Weinzweig." *Fiddlehead* 132 (April 1982): 12-17.

Cowan, Doris. "Interview." *Books in Canada* January 1982: 30-32.

Jenoff, Marvyne. "Helen Weinzweig: Her Life and Work. An Interview." *Waves* 13.4 (Spring 1985): 4-13.

# 3.
# A "Sense of Loss"

## The Fiction of Helen Weinzweig

Helen Weinzweig's interests and career as a fiction writer recall those of George Eliot. Both their works describe contemporary women's struggles as wives, mothers, and daughters, and adapt existing narrative conventions to suit their subjects. Further, Eliot published her first novel, *Adam Bede*, in 1859, when she was forty, and Weinzweig began writing a century later, at the age of forty-five. Despite a delayed beginning, the first works of both writers reveal their originality as well as their artistic maturity. There the similarities end, however, for unlike Eliot, who enjoyed critical recognition during her lifetime, Weinzweig is one of Canada's marginalized writers of fiction.

To date, Helen Weinzweig has published two novels and a collection of short stories. Her marginalization is not so much the result of a relatively small oeuvre but is due largely to the surreal, often bleak vision that informs her writing, a combination that has challenged critics and alienated some readers. The briefest look at Weinzweig's work explains why this is so. Her work betrays an interest in modern painting, music, and, in particular, the French *nouveau roman*. Like the French novelists whom she admires—Alain Robbe-Grillet and Nathalie Sarraute foremost among them—Weinzweig eschews traditional elements such as plot, characterization, and setting as sources of context in her own fiction. Instead, she creates highly visual and fragmented worlds akin to abstract paintings that require the active participation of the reader in assembling the various parts of her literary canvases and interpreting their significance.

Born on 21 May 1915 to Lily (nee Wekselman) and Joseph Tenenbaum in the Polish ghetto of Radom—"a life lived in constant terror of pogroms" (Cowan 31)—Helen Weinzweig emigrated to Canada at the age of nine with her divorced mother. She did not know her father until she was an adult. Weinzweig grew up impoverished and neglected in the Jewish immigrant district of Toronto—now the fashionable Annex neighbourhood—and deliberately abandoned her native Polish and Yiddish languages: "[t]he associations of both were very traumatic for me" (qtd. in Kirchhoff A14). In Toronto, she attended school for the first time and was taught "by wonderful, selfless Presbyterian and Methodist schoolteachers, who knew right from wrong, and who passed on to me the accepted rules of a (then) homogeneous society" (Weinzweig, "Interrupted" 299). In fact, Weinzweig's indigent childhood and adolescence are articulated in her writing as a compelling need to escape the tyranny of poverty and working-class oppression and a pervasive feeling of Jewish cultural malaise. Her mother, who remained a single parent and was sole provider at a time when women rarely found themselves in such circumstances, experienced her share of ill fortune. Weinzweig has described her as "a totally independent woman, who always earned her own living [as a hairdresser], married three times, had live-in male companionship between marriages, had had a number of abortions because she had to support herself and me and her sisters and her father" (Weinzweig, "Interrupted" 297). As a result of her mother's unconventional behaviour, mother and daughter were ostracized from their community as non-conformists. Weinzweig's short story "My Mother's Luck" (later staged as a one-act play and included in the collection *A View from the Roof*), records the difficult life and dynamic character of her mother.

During her adolescence, Weinzweig spent two years at a sanatorium while recuperating from tuberculosis. It was during this period that she developed the love of reading that has continued throughout her life. After completing her junior matriculation at Harbord Collegiate Institute in Toronto, Weinzweig was forced by the Depression to seek employment. She worked as a stenographer, receptionist, and retail sales clerk before marrying the composer John Weinzweig, whom she had met in high school, on 19 July 1940. The marriage lasted sixty-six years, ending with the death of her husband at the age of ninety-three on 24 August 2006.

Weinzweig explains her decision to marry as follows:

> I grew up without a sense of family. Other people had families. So when I married and had my own family, I think I tried to create a family life out of my head. I feel I failed. I still don't know, in other than an intellectual way, what makes a family. So the "sense" of family creeps into my work in a negative way, i.e., what is wrong with this or that family.
>
> I chose the traditional route of marriage and motherhood because I wanted to be accepted by the world around me. Why that was so had a lot to do with my mother. She refused to follow the path of other women.... I decided I would be respectable, and became more so than Caesar's wife. (qtd. in Jenoff 4, 7-8)

Until the age of forty-five, Weinzweig was homemaker and mother to two sons, Paul and Daniel. In addition, she served as chaperone for the National Youth Orchestra of Canada and was an organizer, teacher, and supervisor of a cooperative nursery school in Toronto. Foremost, however, she helped foster her husband's profession; as she admitted herself in 1976, three years following the publication of her first novel, "[b]oth John and I lived his career" ("Weinzweig" 2).

When her children became teenagers and Weinzweig was faced with free time, she suddenly felt unable to read. At the urging of her psychiatrist, who suggested that she begin "to examine things on paper instead of in my head" (qtd. in Kirchhoff A14), she took up writing as a hobby and felt as though she had been "granted a second life" (qtd. in Corbeil 19). She attended a writing course at Ryerson Polytechnical Institute (now Ryerson University) in Toronto and another at Columbia University in New York. She soon began to take her work seriously, particularly when her first story "Surprise!" was published in 1968 in the *Canadian Forum*. Weinzweig's work has never been rejected. Without exception, all her stories and novels were accepted for publication, a significant achievement for one who entered the profession of authorship so late.

Her first novel, *Passing Ceremony*, appeared in 1973 when she was fifty-eight. It was followed by *Basic Black with Pearls* in 1980, Weinzweig's best-known work, which won the City of Toronto Book Award. The novel was published in the United States in 1981. *A View from the Roof*, a collection of thirteen stories written over twenty-one years, was published in 1989 and was also nominated for the Governor General's Literary Award. Her fiction has been translated into French, German, and Italian. The painstaking process of writing and rewriting a novel takes Weinzweig five to six years, which may account for the slim output of a writing career that, despite its late start, now spans thirty years.

A founding member of the Writers' Union of Canada, today Weinzweig is a professional who has held Ontario Arts Council and Canada Council for the Arts grants. In 1978 she received third prize in the CBC Literary Competition for her short story "The Homecoming," and in 1986 she was awarded first prize by Alberta Theatre Productions for "A Classical Education," an unfinished play about her father. In addition, in 1984-85 she was Playwright-in-Residence at Toronto's Tarragon Theatre; and, in 1988-89, Writer-in-Residence at the University of New Brunswick, Fredericton. While she embraces her Jewish background, Weinzweig practices Zen Buddhism. A self-proclaimed feminist, she has been able, through writing, to integrate the conflicting facets of her life.

*Passing Ceremony* introduced Weinzweig's original style and narrative perspective to Canadian readers. The novel is highly experimental in form and presents a sombre, ironic picture of the ritual of marriage, the "passing ceremony" of its title. In its episodic shifts from scene to scene, this brief work draws on cinematic technique. Further, its abstract, visual quality evokes some modern painting. In fact, a painting by the structurist Eli Bornstein that hung in a friend's home—a stark depiction of white, geometrically shaped blocks in seeming random arrangement, yet contained within and unified by the frame—provided the form for *Passing Ceremony*. The novel also adopts the fragmented structure that often characterizes a piece of modern music. Most notably, Weinzweig's fiction reveals the influence of her composer husband's music, which is marked by a "clarity of texture; economy of material; rhythmic energy; tight motivic organization ...; short melodic outbursts contrasted with long flowing lines; and harmonies which, though often harsh, never fully lose their tonal orientation" (Henninger 1392).

*Passing Ceremony* adopts strategies of ellipsis and compression in order to defer continually any possible unity of plot. Weinzweig herself has noted her "short sense of time. I find I use one sentence and try and make it tell everything" (qtd. in Bauer 13). By interspersing third person commentary, dialogue, and interior monologue—without identifying the speaker in each instance—Weinzweig's presentation of character is deliberately fractured. The reader is forced to suspend her judgment of events and individuals until the conclusion of the novel.

As epigraph, the author cites the following passage from Ivy Compton-Burnett's *A Father and His Fate* to set the tone for her work: "'Now what an odd thing the marriage service is!' said Miles, leaning back and using an almost confidential tone 'I have been reading it. And I can hardly believe that I have heard it pronounced over myself. I mean I had forgotten that part of things. It is only a passing ceremony'" (Compton-Burnett 119). Weinzweig treats the marriage ceremony as an absurdity. It no longer signifies the communal sanctioning of two individuals who join together in a vow to sustain and respect one another through life. Instead, we are presented with a hollow ceremony and a wedding celebration attended by a cast of characters who border on the grotesque and who gather, it would seem, only to inflict suffering on one another and themselves.

The conventions of marriage and monogamy are parodied in this black comedy of betrayal. The bride has had a miscarriage and has invited several of her former lovers to the wedding; the groom laments the absence of his former homosexual lover and mourns his sister's suicide. The two marry in an effort to dull the pain of their lives, the result of their desperate seeking after love. The father of the bride brings along his new wife, an eighteen-year-old Mexican woman, and their baby. In doing so, he provokes the bride's mother, now an angry older woman whom he deserted years earlier. There is little action here; instead, individuals whisper among themselves and privately remember the infidelities that have shaped their own and the lives of everyone present. As Peter Buitenhuis has noted, the wedding guests are "bored with the ceremony and trapped in various isolations of ennui, hatred, sickness, fantasy, or self-disgust" (1174).

Whatever unity there is in the novel is provided by event, setting, and time. The wedding ceremony is held in a damp chapel and the celebration that follows takes place in "a gray stone mansion" that resembles "a miniature castle with a turret and spires and a red tiled roof" (Weinzweig, *Passing* 14). The events occupy one day. The reader uses these constants as a foundation on which to build her understanding of ever-changing scenes. Weinzweig's spare prose moves the events along quickly and builds momentously toward an ambiguous but inevitable conclusion:

> Daylight is still feeble at the window when husband and wife stir in wakefulness. They appear to sense one another's intention, for they simultaneously leave the bed, put on their greatcoats and go out from the room. In the shadows of the little hall (someone has turned out the electric light) they whisper:
> Ready?
> Ready. (*Passing* 119-20)

There is no redemption here for either the characters or the reader. As the newly married couple leaves the mansion and enters an emerging dawn and an uncharted future, the ending is grim, abrupt, and ironically unsettling.

As an expressionistic work that dispenses with traditional fictional elements, *Passing Ceremony* employs strategies from other genres—film, painting, and music—to bring unity and meaning to an otherwise broken and senseless world. Weinzweig's nightmarish cynicism remains unique, however, and communicates her belief in the paradox that tragedy always lurks beneath the comfortable and conventional surface of everyday life. For the author, that paradox can only be illuminated by a narrative style that blends the surreal and the gothic, a strong mixture for most readers. Weinzweig herself tells the following anecdote: "After reading my first novel, a man said to me at a party, 'If I were your husband I would hit you'" (Weinzweig, "Interrupted" 300). For those who do relish her work, however, *Passing Ceremony* unquestionably is "a *tour de force* on an unattractive subject" (Buitenhuis 1174)—the failure of human relationships.

*Basic Black with Pearls*, seven years later, is also an ingenious work of puzzles that exposes the vacuousness of traditional marriage, but it is at once more complex and more unified than the earlier novel. Like its predecessor, *Basic Black with Pearls* obliges the reader to work her way through several layers of textual significance. Three central concerns of Weinzweig's second novel, which add "a zany sense of humour to her considerable talents for surrealism" (Klovan 136), are the restricted and subservient lives of women, the weight of the past on the present, and, as she says, "the crazy ... house of appearance and illusion" (Weinzweig, "Personal" 363). Its protagonist is the respectable Shirley Kaszenbowski, nee Silverberg, alias Lola Montez,[1] a middle-class, middle-aged, married woman in a basic black dress and pearls who travels the world to meet her elusive lover, Coenraad, an alleged spy for an unidentified "Agency."

Begun when she was in her sixties, Weinzweig was seeking a female-gendered narrative form that would articulate the sense of depersonalization and fragmentation experienced by women of her generation who felt trapped in marriages and prescribed roles that were unfulfilling. Written as a highly subjective interior monologue, the author's experimentation with narrative voice in the novel gave her unexpected difficulty.[2] She had set out to create

> one of those "search" adventures towards self-realization, written in the first person. The hardest part of the writing was learning to use the first person singular. It was then that I was shocked into admitting that I rarely said "I" except in apology or explanation. I, the writer, had to decide what the fictional "I" knew; what did the "I" feel; what did the "I" think; how did the "I" respond ...? ("Interrupted" 299)

Well into the novel the reader learns that Shirley—the "I" of the text—is either schizophrenic or has suffered a nervous breakdown. This revelation raises the possibility of madness and calls into question the authenticity of Shirley's narrative—is it real or imagined?

The epigraph from Ann Quin's *Passages* signals the novel's interest in the relationship between reality and illusion: "I asked him to take off his mask, but this is all I have, he replied. Take it off I commanded. He did so. It's no use I still cannot recognise you—put the mask back on—there that's better now that I know I don't know you we can talk more easily" (Quin 106). Disguise is at the heart of *Basic Black with Pearls*. Shirley Kaszenbowski dons the alias of Lola Montez to protect her own and Coenraad's identities. Her tailored tweed coat, black dress, and pearls are the costume of middle-class respectability and falsely suggest prosperity, stability, and status. Francesca, the woman who replaces Shirley in her own household, wears the latter's "black jersey dress ... held up by bony shoulders and pulled together at the waist by a man's brown leather belt" (Weinzweig, *Basic* 122). As wife and stepmother, Francesca is uncannily familiar as Shirley's double; prior to her flight from conformity, Shirley lived according to the same code of conventional behaviour that now regulates Francesca's existence. Further, Shirley does not know what Coenraad looks like since he always meets her in disguise and their time together is brief. As she says:

> It was true that officially I did not exist. My passport bore a false name. No one but Coenraad knew my whereabouts. Since I was no longer domiciled I did not appear on voters' lists. I was a stranger in the midst of strangers. Not for me the comfort of being recognized by the company I keep. Yet this solitary life had its advantages: if no one cared about me, I need please no one. Except my lover. (80)

Shirley's chameleon-like transformations, the ease with which Francesca adopts the part of Shirley, and Coenraad's apparently endless number of disguises imply that all behaviour is mere play-acting. The author's innovative use of the mask motif heightens the interplay of reality and illusion that is at the heart of this text.

Weinzweig's novel is a complex interlacing of three narrative layers and an overt attempt to displace narrative continuity. First, as Lola Montez, the narrator tells of her long-time affair with Coenraad and their numerous rendezvous around the globe. Second, the narrative moves back in time as Shirley Silverberg describes her youth spent in the poor, Jewish immigrant district of Toronto. Finally, Shirley Kaszenbowski recounts the circumstances of her everyday life as the model Jewish wife of her Polish husband, Zbigniew, and the mother of their children, Anton and Dina. Connecting these narrative layers is Shirley's present search for Coenraad, which returns her to Toronto and several of the city's Elm Streets where she can don an identity of her own choosing.

*Basic Black with Pearls* adopts the scenic structure of Weinzweig's first novel. Unlike the earlier work, however, in which scenic presentation fractures the narrative and defers coherence, in the later text five scenes unify events, which follow a cyclical rather than a sequential pattern. In his study of the novel, critic Bernard Selinger identifies its principal scenes as (1) Silk Factory (pp. 32-39); (2) Bakery (pp. 43-50); (3) Art Gallery (pp. 54-59); (4) Elsie's Mother (pp. 80-84); and (5) Bluebeard (pp. 43-50). Selinger shows that each scene "contains at least one flight to the past" (41). Although each main scene leads to another, the text evades the cause and effect pattern that plot traditionally provides. Instead, a cyclical narrative structure parallels Shirley's wandering from one Elm Street to another, the novel's governing action. In fact, structurally the work operates as small cyclical narratives framed by a large cyclical action of flight. The form suggests the cycle of the female body, by which women are defined in the text.

Shirley seeks to escape the past of her childhood and youth, her marriage to Zbigniew, and finally, her relationship with Coenraad. In the end, however, the novel asserts the stranglehold of the past on the present and Shirley is "free" only to begin another affair. Whether or not the final flight to Andy, Shirley's latest lover, represents a turning point in her life remains deliberately ambiguous. Like *Passing Ceremony*, which concludes uncertainly, *Basic Black with Pearls* does not presume to map its protagonist's future. The text ends not in resolution but in flight, which, by 1980, was already a Weinzweig trademark.

Moreover, the question of veracity—whether Shirley's story is authentic or fabricated—is not answered by the novel. Instead, the approximation of reality and illusion remains a concern of the work to the end. Structurally, the author blurs the boundaries of perception in an attempt to subvert novelistic conventions. Thematically, she does so to reveal the interplay of appearance and illusion in women's lives. In the end, whether Shirley has told the "truth" or has imagined her story out of madness is not the reader's primary concern. Rather, one is impressed with the work's technical precision and its examination of women's enforced passivity in a patriarchal world. Shirley escapes from a hollow, unlived life only to begin a relationship with Andy, yet another stranger in a series of estranged partners. That Weinzweig could not offer her protagonist a different script is troubling to readers and author alike:

> The ending was a problem that held me up for almost a year. I could find no solution for this woman who leaves home—whether she leaves home physically or mentally is not the point. But she does leave her occupation, which is wife and mother, and goes out into the big world. And I couldn't find anything for her to do out in that big world. That question has disturbed me as a person and as a writer. (qtd. in Bauer 15)

*Basic Black with Pearls* is a provoking work that challenges readers' assumptions about women's roles as well as narrative conventions. The text invites a range of responses: some appreciate its dark humour, while others regard it as a psychotic account.[3] However one reads *Basic Black with Pearls*, it is a skillful and powerful novel that brought Weinzweig critical acclaim, a wider audience for her distinctive style and haunting vision, and confirmed her as a master of surrealistic fiction.

Following the publication of her second novel, the author turned briefly from writing to theatrical work. In May 1983, "My Mother's Luck," a story that first appeared in *Jewish Dialog* in 1977, was staged in Toronto as a one-act play. Part of Factory Theatre Lab's Brave New Works series, it featured Pol Pelletier in an extended monologue of an indomitable, unsentimental woman—a character based on Weinzweig's mother—who "was battered by the forces of European history and shaped by a disproportionate amount of 'bad luck with weak men'" (Corbeil 19). Addressing her silent daughter,

Weinzweig's character speaks an idiosyncratic English, redolent of Yiddish syntax, colloquialisms, and expressions, which makes the text particularly adaptable to an oral and visual medium. This was Weinzweig's first story to be dramatized, and seeing Pelletier's performance proved cathartic for the writer. A testimony to her mother's suffering, the daughter found her own work difficult to witness as theatre. The story later formed part of "A View from the Roof," a theatrical piece based on three of Weinzweig's stories, adapted for the stage by Dave Carley and performed at Toronto's Tarragon Theatre in June 1996.

"My Mother's Luck" was included in the collection of short stories also titled *A View from the Roof*. In fact, all of the stories included in the volume were published previously. "The Homecoming," for example, appeared as the final pages of *Basic Black with Pearls* and "Causation," one of the finest stories in the collection, appears here for the sixth time. As reviewer Kenneth Radu states, however, the repetition does not detract from the value of the collection, which he regards as equal in many respects to the writing of Mavis Gallant (80).

The stories are grouped thematically rather than chronologically, an appropriate arrangement since the material was written over a span of twenty-one years. The first eight stories record the clash of Jews and Gentiles, while the latter five stories are more obviously experimental. Many of the concerns in this collection are familiar from the novels. A controlling theme is the power of memory and how it shapes—and often distorts—one's present and future life. Many of Weinzweig's protagonists are of European Jewish background and their personal histories are burdened with memories of Hitler and his reign of terror. A preoccupation with marriage is evident in the number of stories about couples who are locked in stultifying relationships. Women are victims in these marriages, but Weinzweig's male characters do not fare much better in narratives that detail the agonizing "business of living" (Sullivan 24). The author reveals an abiding interest in art and music, recurring motifs in the stories. Moreover, narrative experiment and an impersonal tone, punctuated by flashes of humour, are characteristic of the collection and recognizable to readers of the novels.

Memory is a common thread in these stories. In "The Means,"

the narrator Margaret uses a stranger she meets in an Arlesian restaurant to help exorcise the painful memories of her father, who abandoned his daughter and his Jewish wife at the start of the Second World War, and of Raoul, a passing acquaintance whom she had met twenty-five years earlier in Marseilles. Here, memory is the justification for the narrator's ruthless seduction of an innocent, accommodating man. Similarly, in "L'Envoi," the narrator's memory of her mother's traumatic separation from her family at the age of nine influences our reading of the daughter's own story, which forms the larger part of the text. The neglected wife of an artist, she seeks refuge in a relationship with her husband's best friend. As she claims, "my entire life has been spent trying to forge one human tie with one person in this whole wide world who would want me" (Weinzweig, *View* 116). Throughout the volume, the reader encounters desolate characters whose lives have been misshapen by their memories and who are absorbed by the unnerving power of recollection: "Memory ... can be disturbing, since memory and emotion often go together, sometimes to no apparent purpose, so why permit memories to intrude on one's life?" (112). In Weinzweig's fictional world, informed by the author's Jewish sensibility and keen awareness of the atrocities of the Second World War, the intrusion of memory into daily life is inevitable.

Relationships between men and women are scrutinized in these stories that expose love as false and pretentious. "Causation" records the loveless connections between one woman and two men, the first her former husband, the second a fascist gigolo. In this tale of mutual abuse, the characters are motivated by selfish needs. By paying alimony and allowing her to live in his house, Oswald controls his ex-wife; in the hope of eventually inheriting her wealth, Gyorgi seduces the older woman; and she, a former opera star, now depends economically and sexually on both men. "A View from the Roof" also tells of a woman's sterile relationship with two men. While she and her husband, Bernard, are attending an academic conference in San Juan, Betty Adelman has a fleeting affair with Mauricio Sulano, a painter. Betty's ordinary existence as a faculty wife is disrupted temporarily by her liaison with Sulano, who, despite his artistic posturing, proves as self-interested and facile as the husband she finds so tedious. Betty's rage at the conclusion of the story is symptomatic of Weinzweig's female characters who are forced to repress their memories and their emotions, often at the cost of their sanity.

Weinzweig's fascination with art and music is evident throughout the collection. Her artist figures are all male and they are relentless in their pursuit of artistic material. Many of her female characters are either married to or romantically involved with artists whose love of self is paramount and who attribute little value to their personal relationships. In "Journey to Porquis," for example, a writer flees the demands of his wife and children and takes fictional refuge aboard a train that never reaches a final destination. "What Happened to Ravel's Bolero?" subverts the conventions of romantic love that *Bolero* celebrates. The story repeats the same sentences with slight variations and builds in intensity, much like the musical composition. In fact, it adapts the twelve-tone serialism of John Weinzweig, the first Canadian composer to employ the technique. Weinzweig's serialism explores the same twelve notes through an arrangement of intervals and rhythmic irregularities, in order to achieve an aesthetic and emotional effect. In Helen Weinzweig's similarly pioneering prose style, serial technique heightens the reader's experience and comprehension of a love affair between a middle-aged, married man and a young, single woman.[4]

The second issue of *Parchment*, a journal devoted to contemporary Canadian Jewish writing, includes a story by Weinzweig entitled "The Sea at Bar." Like her other short fiction, it explores the torturous effects of memory and the toll it takes on one's life. The Jewish male protagonist of this tale describes the experience of having been hidden in the home of a Gentile during the Second World War, when he was an adolescent. Sheltered by a one-time princess, he was required to repay her generosity by impregnating her. Despite the kind treatment he received, the story illuminates the emotional and psychological harm that results when one is torn from one's roots, forced to deny one's true self, obliged to submit to another's demands, and used as a pawn to secure one's life.

Like the novels, Weinzweig's stories lack resolution. Their inconclusive endings always surprise, often shock, the reader and that effect is deliberate. The author aims to shatter the notion that literature ought to affirm and reflect life as her readers conceive it.

She draws a scalpel across each page and makes careful incisions into the lives of her characters. In doing so, she lays bare the suffering and "sense of loss" (Jenoff 12) that has shaped them, and attains a closer correlation between life and art than realistic fiction could ever achieve—for her readers recognize as their own the faces of her characters and the painful hollowness of their lives.

Weinzweig's accomplishment as an author of great skill and insight is no small achievement, especially for one who turned to writing at the age of forty-five. She quickly perfected her craft as an avant-garde writer whose work in English is modeled after the French *nouveau roman*. The spareness of her style camouflages the intensity, drama, and depth of her fictional worlds, peopled, as they often are, with broken, dispossessed characters who desperately seek meaning in their lives. As a writer, two of Weinzweig's greatest contributions have been to expose and condemn the constrained lives of women of her generation, and to probe their sense of depersonalization. Having begun her career late, the author is not hampered by the demands of a publisher since, as she has said, "all I've got is time" (qtd. in Bauer 17). In fact, hers is a fiction of process and integrity that does not presume to offer solutions. Rather, Weinzweig remains faithful to her belief that writing is a "voyage of discovery that takes a long time" (qtd. in Bauer 17).

## Notes

[1] Lola Montez (1818-61) was the pseudonym of the Irish-born actress Maria Dolores Eliza Rosanna Gilbert. She was involved in an early scandalous divorce, following which she toured the Continent as a dancer. In 1847 she became the official mistress of Ludwig I of Bavaria but her liberal sympathies led to his abdication and her banishment. Later she toured the United States as a ballet dancer and actress. In California she acted in a sketch of her own life, "Lola Montez in Bavaria." She was famous for her beauty and as "the international bad girl of the mid-Victorians" (see Hart 559).
[2] A number of critics have noted the metafictional aspects of *Basic Black with Pearls*. Rachel Feldhay Brenner, for example, reads the novel as "indeed Shirley's [own] story based on memories of her affair with Coenraad." And Weinzweig herself has said, "I disturb

the reader. He's not quite sure what's going on, and he wants to feel adequate to the situation so he will turn the page to find out.... The reader participates in the writing process." See Brenner 30; and Bauer 13-14.

[3] S. R. MacGillivray and Noreen Ivancic, for example, comment as follows on Weinzweig's novels: "The quite bizarre wedding that serves as the focal point of *Passing Ceremony* gradually reveals itself as the grotesquerie of an asylum where all are inmates. Shirley Kaszenbowski's on-going world-wide quest for the ever-elusive Coenraad in *Basic Black with Pearls* may be, for all the credible anchoring detail of each 'episode,' only the imaginative flights of fancy of a woman confined to a mental hospital" (227).

[4] For an analysis of Weinzweig's use of serialism see MacGillivray and Ivancic.

**Works Cited**

Bauer, Nancy. "Nancy Bauer Interviews Helen Weinzweig." *Fiddlehead* 132 (April 1982): 12-17.

Brenner, Rachel Feldhay. "The Reader as a Private Eye: Rediscovering the Author in Helen Weinzweig's 'Basic Black with Pearls.'" *Ariel* 20.2 (April 1989): 21-38.

Buitenhuis, Peter. "Weinzweig, Helen." *The Oxford Companion to Canadian Literature*. Ed. William Toye. 2nd ed. Toronto: Oxford University Press, 1983. 1174.

Compton-Burnett, Ivy. *A Father and His Fate*. London: Gollancz, 1957.

Corbeil, Carole. "Theatrical Venture a Meeting of the Minds." *Globe and Mail* 4 May 1983: 19.

Cowan, Doris. "Interview." *Books in Canada* Jan. 1982: 30-32.

Hart, James D. *The Oxford Companion to American Literature*. 4th ed. New York: Oxford University Press, 1965. 559.

Henninger, Richard, and John Beckwith. "Weinzweig, John." *Encyclopedia of Music in Canada*. Eds. Helmut Kallman, Gilles Potvin, and Kenneth Winters. 2nd ed. Toronto: University of Toronto Press, 1992. 1391-94.

Jenoff, Marvyne. "Helen Weinzweig: Her Life and Work. An Interview." *Waves* 13.4 (Spring 1985): 4-13.

Kirchhoff, H. J. "Quirky Imagination, Hard Work Spell Success for Writer." *Globe and Mail* 7 March 1990: A14.

Klovan, Peter. "Canadian Gothic." Rev. of *Basic Black with Pearls*, by Helen Weinzweig; and *Gentle Sinners*, by W. D. Valgardson. *Canadian Literature* 88 (Spring 1981): 136-38.

MacGillivray, S. R. and Noreen Ivancic. "'What Happened to Ravel's *Bolero*?': Weinzweig's Serialism." *English Studies in Canada* 17.2 (June 1991): 225-34.

Quin, Ann. *Passages*. London: Calder and Boyars, 1969.

Radu, Kenneth. "The Last Word." Rev. of *Nice Work*, by David Lodge; *Gilles & Jeanne*, by Michel Tournier; and *A View from the Roof*, by Helen Weinzweig. *Matrix* 31 (Spring-Summer 1990): 79-80.

Selinger, Bernard. "Every Reader a Writer: Helen Weinzweig's *Basic Black with Pearls*." *Essays on Canadian Writing* 36 (Spring 1988): 38-56.

Sullivan, Rosemary. "Cast a Cold Eye." Rev. of *A View from the Roof*, by Helen Weinzweig. *Books in Canada* Dec. 1989: 24-25.

Weinzweig, Helen. *Basic Black with Pearls*. Toronto: House of Anansi Press, 1980.

Weinzweig, Helen. "The Interrupted Sex." *Language in Her Eye: Views on Writing and Gender by Canadian Women Writing in English*. Eds. Libby Scheier, Sarah Sheard, and Eleanor Wachtel. Toronto: Coach House Press, 1990. 297-301.

Weinzweig, Helen. "My Mother's Luck." *Jewish Dialog* (Passover 1977): 4-8.

Weinzweig, Helen. *Passing Ceremony*. Toronto: Anansi, 1973.

Weinzweig, Helen. "Personal Note." *Canada Writes! The Members' Book of the Writers' Union of Canada*. Ed. K. A. Hamilton. Toronto: Writers' Union of Canada, 1977. 362-63.

Weinzweig, Helen. "The Sea at Bar." *Parchment: Contemporary Canadian Jewish Writing* 2 (1993-94): 11-18.

Weinzweig, Helen. "Surprise!" *Canadian Forum* March 1968: 276-79.

Weinzweig, Helen. *A View from the Roof*. Fredericton: Goose Lane Editions, 1989.

"Weinzweig: The Late-Blooming Novelist." *Saturday Night* October 1976: 2.

# 4.
# Close to the Bone

Woman's Place in Nora Gold's *Marrow and Other Stories*

Nora Gold's debut collection *Marrow and Other Stories* (1998) probes women's lives as they are framed and shaped by the patriarchal culture and practice of Judaism. Gold surveys personal relationships as volatile, political terrain, and her fiction is imbued with a palpable ideology—Zionist with a leftist slant. Faith and heritage are important in her stories that variously challenge and embrace the rites of passage available to Jewish women. *Marrow* provocatively, and perhaps more explicitly than the other works under consideration in this volume, condemns the constraints of Judaism, rejects the protective veil Judaism offers women, and only fleetingly celebrates its gift of spirituality.

Born and raised in Montreal, Nora Gold now lives in Toronto and is a former professor of social work at McMaster University in nearby Hamilton; she spends part of each year in Israel. A deep, abiding Zionism informs her sharp evocation of a country torn by political infighting. Her writing reflects her firsthand knowledge of the little explored corners of women's private lives. Like Saskatchewan writer Joanne Gerber, whose startling collection *In the Misleading Absence of Light* (1997) details the trauma of women who seek spiritual solace from the same Church that excludes them, Gold describes women betrayed by Judaism. In focusing on women, in particular "modern intellectuals imbued with a Jewish tradition that is sometimes difficult to reconcile with their lives in contemporary [North] America" (Shapiro 2), she reveals how their need for inclusion is thwarted by a religion that refuses them full participation.

A careful, spare writer, Gold eschews dense and detailed description in favour of blunt and powerful language. She brings the same precision to characterization: she draws women deftly and economically. Often the briefest comment provides the context necessary to understand a character and her circumstance. Gold's women are introspective, but they are not given to self-analysis. Rather, insights—when they arrive—come and go swiftly, usually with little result, and her accurate mirroring of lived experience is poignant.

The reader's discomfort is increased by a hollowness, felt as a "permanent state of impermanence" (Glazer, "Orphans" 131), that resonates throughout *Marrow* and resides at the core of Gold's characters, many of whom have just reached forty, the magical "middle" age that, in North American culture, appears to have particular significance for women. Across the collection, the unwilling passage into one's forties marks the final loss of youth for women whose irrevocable entry into adulthood is usually painful. Many endure the loss of love, either the death of a loved one or the demise of a relationship, and the remaining void is a morbid wound. Despite successful careers, Gold's protagonists are traditional women who seek intimacy through marriage and children. When marriage and children provide little comfort, as they generally do, there is nothing left to satisfy their lingering desire for personal connection. In spite of glimmerings of hope, Gold's fictional landscapes are almost bereft of redemption.

This absence of redemption in Gold's stories is all the more striking given her interest in Judaism and Israel. In fact, the irony in her fiction is felt most keenly in the empty centres of women's lives where, she makes clear, Judaism fails to meet their needs. Invariably, they are forsaken by a religious tradition that Miriyam Glazer describes as "ambivalent at best, exclusionary at worst, towards females in general" ("Daughters" 83). Despite real efforts to discover a place for themselves within their faith, these women "face absence rather than presence" when they turn their "attention to Judaism or to Jewish culture and history" (Glazer, "Orphans" 128), and are frustrated with the marginal opportunities for self-expression within Judaism and their private lives. When spiritual and professional malaise combine—several women lose interest in their work—darkness descends.

The title story sets the tone for the volume. A visibly pregnant Hannah is visiting Israel with her husband and son. In error, the family drives through an Arab part of old Jerusalem when a boy wielding a slingshot attacks their car. The family is not injured, but there is "a huge jagged wound in the rear window" (Gold 12) of their vehicle. Two days later, once husband and son have returned to Canada while Hannah remains in Israel for a conference, she begins to hemorrhage and is admitted to hospital. There, as she delivers a dead fetus and is attended by an Orthodox Jew whose views she abhors, Hannah recognizes the essential loneliness of her marriage.

A piercing, clipped narrative—"She lost her baby in Hebrew. That is, she lost her baby in a hospital in a foreign language. That is, she can't talk about the death of that baby since it happened in Hebrew, in a language that made no sense" (Gold 9)—introduces the dominant motifs of the collection: the female body out of control, death of a loved one, the emptiness of marriage, the political factions in Israel, and the patriarchy of Orthodoxy. Told in the third person, as are most of Gold's stories, Hannah is denied her first-person voice that would bring intimacy to the telling. This distanced narrative perspective dominates the collection, heightening the "sense of marginalization, alienation, [and] disempowerment" (Glazer, "Orphans" 131) among women that Gold is determined to articulate.

Hannah is typical of Gold's protagonists. A successful professional, she is married and has a young son. Despite outward appearances, she is unhappy and recalls the intimacy and "indolent" (Gold 12) love she once shared with a young Israeli man. The distant past—a time when Israel knew peace and Hannah knew love—resonates throughout "Marrow," with its focus on the religious and political divisions that threaten present-day Israel, on Hannah's lonely marriage, and on the death of her second child in utero, a loss that she must face alone in a foreign country. The title story, moreover, introduces Gold's penchant for economy and precision: its incisive rendering of a desolate woman is achieved in seven pages.

In "Miniatures," a story consisting of separate vignettes, Gold sketches eight women on their fortieth birthday, a momentous event in each of their lives. Of the eight, only three are content: one adores a loving husband, a second shares a picnic lunch with a close woman friend, a third gazes at her reflection and, finding herself beautiful, for the first time "feels a sudden desire to be faithful … to this face in the mirror, to this woman" (Gold 43). The others are drifters, desperate to find meaning at middle age amid the debris of multiple miscarriages, unrequited love, overwhelming loneliness, fierce anger, and incipient madness. One woman, for example, is struggling with anorexia and another is mourning a miscarriage:

> Her third dead baby, one born every spring.
> [S]he wonders what springtime feels like, *real* spring, spring without a baby to mourn. She can't remember. She tries to imagine a spring without blood surprising her on underwear, on the floors of restaurants, filling up toilets. She can't. Springtime now is the time that babies die: It is life hanging by a thin bloody thread, and then unravelling like poor knitting. (Gold 34)

For Gold's protagonists, the watershed age of forty brings no respite from anguish, loneliness, and self-loathing. Instead, it engenders a debilitating crisis of identity.

Even the lone woman satisfied in her marriage recognizes it "is not fashionable, it is not politically correct, in the circles in which she moves, to admit this; so she will whisper it: *I love my husband*" (Gold 33). In whispering—she feels unable to proclaim publicly her pleasure in marriage—the narrator admits of love's tenuousness in the brutalizing, day-to-day world. With a skillful touch that focuses on slight detail, Gold provides telling glimpses into the emotional range of women in response to their bodies, in relationships with men, in friendships with other women, and in private moments with themselves.

Gold's interest in the unglamorous lives of middle-aged career women sets her apart from other writers who frequently focus on the struggles of younger women. Her fiction is distinguished further by its emphasis on the "spiritual thirst" (Glazer, "Will" 126) of Jewish women. Today, when spirituality often is equated with the New Age, it is refreshing to read stories of women who seek fulfilment through traditional religious practice. Unfortunately, in *Marrow* these efforts are frustrated by a faith and culture that regularly displace rather than embrace the female experience, confirming Jewish women's "still-vivid memory of their long exclusion from participation in the central religious rites" (Glazer, "Will" 126) of Judaism.

In "Yosepha," a contemporary retelling of the biblical story of Joseph, who is recast here as female, the protagonist is betrayed by her siblings and forced to fend for herself. Gifted with a spiritual, "eerie way of seeing right through to the essence of a thing" (Gold 122), Yosepha is her father's favourite. Brought to the desert and abandoned there by her jealous siblings, Yosepha grows up thinking that her father has forsaken her as well. As an adult, she is reconciled with the family she has not seen for twenty-two years and finally learns that her father never knew of his children's treachery. Enduring loyalty and professional success—Yosepha now heads Israel's Ministry of Agriculture—allows her to transcend her own suffering and assist her destitute family. Her quick willingness to forgive, however, rings hollow in the face of past abuse and her reasoning—"I will take care of you—you are my family" (132)—suggests that she is more biblical figure than contemporary character (despite her professional achievement) and cannot be considered among Gold's usual protagonists who feel the deep and abiding suffering of early abandonment.

Gold levels her greatest indictment against Judaism in the powerful story "The Lesson of the Rabbi." An adolescent girl escapes an unhappy home by taking refuge with her rabbi and his family. A brilliant student, she devotes herself to her studies with the rabbi, a charismatic and loving figure who nurtures Carla's trust only to shatter it later, when she is most fragile and alone. The sexual nature of the rabbi's touch—physical contact is forbidden to Orthodox Jews prior to marriage and also smacks of adultery in this story—makes his violation all the more menacing. By the end of the narrative, Carla is utterly bereft; she realizes "there will be no more safety, and no more fathers, and no more hope for her, ever again. She knows now that the world is godless and empty, and there will be no redemption, not through the body, and not through the mind" (Gold 78). In this godless world, female characters who surrender themselves to men of "faith" are traumatized.

Like Yosepha, Carla is young when she first experiences betrayal. She is neglected by parents too self-absorbed to notice their exceptional daughter; their hollow marriage taints Carla and her brothers, as well as husband and wife. Later, the rabbi who spurs her curiosity and inspires her faith in Judaism, challenges her precocious intelligence, welcomes her into his home, and accepts her as a daughter is the same man who sucks her fingers in his kitchen in a macabre moment of sexual awakening for Carla.

In fact, throughout *Marrow* girls and women are vulnerable to men who wield a terrifying authority. The lack of protection for women, and the dearth of mother figures to care for characters such as Carla or Yosepha, is striking and departs from Judaism's sanctioning of women as nurturers. Gold's protagonists are denied the guidance and love that mothers can offer their daughters. Carla's mother, for example, criticizes her "ceaselessly on everything from her posture to her grammar" (Gold 65) and Yosepha's mother, Rachel, rejects her at birth. Having set her heart on a "prince[ly]" (117) son, Rachel shuns her newborn daughter's cries and dies soon after giving birth. In story after story, mothers are bored, self-consumed, and inept, callous, hateful, or altogether absent. In place of mothers as guides, Gold offers fathers, husbands, lovers, brothers, and rabbis who invariably prove lethal. Repeatedly, women misplace their trust in emotionally distant men who become unsatisfactory partners. As Eve tells Pearl in "Flesh," the novella that concludes the volume, "If you want to know how to turn love into hate, I can tell you how to do it.... Just marry the guy" (206).

In Gold's stories, women frequently are brutalized or abandoned, their lives shattered within the patriarchal framework of male-female relationships and Judaism. Unable to sustain meaningful connections, they internalize a deep-rooted suffering. In the only first-person narrative included in the collection, "Final Movement," an unnamed female narrator, whose sickly mother dies too early to proffer protection, recounts in a disembodied voice the vacuousness of her own marriage and a one-night encounter with a former acquaintance. She describes the demise of a friend's marriage with the same aloofness she brings to personal experience.

The motif of death, prominent across the collection, surfaces in this story to return the narrator to her hometown of Winnipeg, Manitoba. Here, as she settles her aunt's estate, she revisits people and places of her youth. Married for a long time, she and her husband are childless, a loss she once felt keenly and to which she attributes the emptiness of her relationship. The lack of intimacy in her marriage impels the narrator to seek out Henry Hailik, a former schoolmate with whom she has a brief liaison. It is Henry who offers the startling revelation—"as though it were nothing, just a minor piece of gossip" (Gold 102)—that so disturbs the narrator: that the husband of a former friend is an adulterer.

Over many years, to assuage her own sadness, the narrator has nourished the ideal of her friend's happy marriage. The shattering of that illusion has a profound impact on her: "[I]t was the end of something, the breaking off of a piece of my world. Nothing is ever going to be all right again, nothing will ever be intact" (Gold 102). The narrator is devastated at the tarnishing of the great romance she has cherished and idealized since youth. The union of Ruth Barron and Tom Combes has been the touchstone she has relied on throughout the cold days of her own marriage. The love that brought together the beautiful and privileged Ruth and her talented composer husband sustained the narrator who has clung fervently to the romantic ideal of "one woman—one man" (Radway 123), even when her own experience of love differed markedly from her fantasy. Despite her recent affair with Henry, the narrator cannot accept "triangular relationships" (Radway 123) in the marriage of Ruth and Tom. Her fantasy defiled, she is moved to ire: "I hate how men can do this, how men have the power to do this, to do whatever they want with women" (Gold 102). In "Final Movement," Gold unveils the psychic scarring that results from a painful severing of emotional and physical ties.

The gaping divide between emotional and physical selves is another motif throughout the volume, rendered most poignantly in the story of Pearl, an anorexic and agoraphobic who is mourning the recent death of her mother. Withdrawn as a child and witness to her father's angry abuse, she remains immature and blames her mother (with whom she always has lived) for her suffering. After a brief and belated relationship with an out-of-town visitor (when she is forty-one and still virginal), Pearl constructs an elaborate, adolescent fantasy in which her lover returns to her and proposes marriage. When he fails to do so, Pearl clings more resolutely than ever to the hermitic life she has chosen and nearly starves herself to death. Unequipped with the emotional armour of Gold's other protagonists, Pearl is least able to function in the "real" world but is most connected to her inner self.

As an anorexic, Pearl is adolescent in body; as a recluse who challenges a nurturing mother, she also is adolescent in her behaviour. In calling, however, for total separation of the female self from the outside "male" sphere, "Flesh" is charged with a breathtaking irony. The terrific cost paid by women who attempt to fit themselves into an unaccommodating world is made especially clear in this final story. Eve, Pearl's cousin and confidante, admits that despite her own professional and personal success—like many of Gold's characters, she has a career (as a practicing psychologist) and a family of her own—"I don't know where I belong. Maybe nowhere—just going up and down this staircase for the rest of my life. Like the angel on Jacob's ladder, going back and forth eternally between heaven and the earth" (Gold 220). Neither Eve, who lives a seemingly integrated life, nor Pearl, who seeks isolation, finds safe haven in a world of men's making.

In "The Prayer," Laura still is mourning her husband who died prematurely after one year of marriage. Laura is among the privileged, however. Her marriage was harmonious, she and her husband were compatible, and they shared a deep love: "his good-natured, easy-going way, his loose grin sprawled over everything, over their whole life together" (Gold 19-20). Impulsively, and in the wake of Michael's death, Laura begins an affair with his best friend and avows "she has never felt such desire in all her life" (25). Overtaken by physical need, Laura feels dissociated from the inner self she shared so briefly with her husband. Throughout *Marrow*, women are unmoored by trauma that engenders a splitting off of their physical and emotional selves. Often, Gold's protagonists are unable to regain their equilibrium; Laura, however, is an important exception. After leading the High Holiday services at her synagogue on Yom Kippur, the Day of Atonement and the holiest day of the year—the only woman among five people to do so in this Reform congregation—Laura comes to terms with her loss and can open herself to "the incredible joy of being alive" (31).

In its gentle offering of renewal, this story stands out among the others in the collection. Significantly, redemption is achieved through prayer which Orthodox practice always denies women. As Ann Shapiro confirms, "many traditional Talmudists prohibit women from reading ... sacred texts" (8). Here, Laura transcends this restriction by assuming the male role of cantor, "half-man. ... But always a part of her remaining a woman, too" (Gold 28). "The Prayer" signals the need for Judaism to include rather than exclude the female—to the betterment of the larger congregation and the individual woman. In Gold's uncertain and hostile world where women feel severed from themselves and from others, prayer becomes an invaluable vehicle for reconnection.

Gold's characters question their spiritual connection to Judaism. They also appear caught between generations: too young to have broken with traditional expectations for women and too old to have embraced the heady fever of radical feminism, their lives are rife with conflict and attempts to balance marriage, children, and work always fail. At first glance, their hopes for themselves and others appear reasonable, but a closer reading reveals an impractical clinging to romance—an ideal shaped by patriarchal convention—as the source of personal despair.

As Janice Radway explains in *Reading the Romance: Women, Patriarchy, and Popular Literature*, the drive "to achieve *female* selfhood in the romance ... is an expression of patriarchal culture" in which women "realize an identity in relation" to others, as a "self-in-relation" (147). With "its resolute focus on a single, developing relationship" and its eventual resolving of differences between a man and a woman (Radway 122), romance becomes "a utopian wish-fulfillment fantasy through which women try to imagine themselves ... as happy" (Radway 151). Like the women surveyed by Radway for her study, Gold's protagonists believe in the possibility of romance. Either they yearn for a former love now idealized, or they hope for romance to brighten their cheerless lives. In spite of their privileged upbringing, education, and professional status, these women cleave to the ideal of romance as a redemptive source of contentment, a means perhaps to reconcile their conflicted identities as Jewish women living with restrictive traditions.

In a world where women face unspeakable and repeated betrayal by men, however, romance, marriage, and monogamy prove untenable. In the end, thwarted romantic desire, coupled with an inability to attain spiritual fulfilment, leaves Gold's characters feeling unsubstantial and alone. Only Laura is compensated with spiritual comfort, achieved at great cost indeed, for in her cantorial performance as "half-male" she must disavow a true desire to partake fully in Judaism as a woman, as herself.

The Jewish American writer Esther Broner asserts: "[There is] a renewed spiritual quest among women; … we are all looking to remake our mythic past. … [A]nd we are changing the myths to include ourselves.… [W]e are the rediscoverers and the revisionists of a tradition; … [and] we're also doing an enormous amount of new work" (qtd. in Hoy 255, 259, 268). Opposed in voice—raised variously "in anger and in song" (Shapiro 10)—Gold's stories seek to "recapture the spiritual and the religious dimension of Judaism" (Goodman 273) from the perspective of women's experience. In so doing, her fiction mines "the substance and the contours" (Glazer, "Will" 127) of contemporary women's lives. Gold's art dignifies her characters as thoughtful, articulate women who aspire to satisfying relationships, spiritual engagement, and a sense of personal well-being. For Nora Gold, a "multiple, changeable, fluid" (Antler xiv) identity as a Jew, a North American, and a woman serves as valuable impetus for her writing.

**Works Cited**

Antler, Joyce. *The Journey Home: Jewish Women and the American Century*. New York: Free Press, 1997.

Gerber, Joanne. *In the Misleading Absence of Light*. Regina: Coteau, 1997.

Glazer, Miriyam. "'Daughters of Refugees of the Ongoing-Universal-Endless-Upheaval': Anne Roiphe and the Quest for Narrative Power in Jewish American Women's Fiction." *Daughters of Valor: Contemporary Jewish American Women Writers*. Eds. Jay L. Halio and Ben Siegel. Newark: University of Delaware Press, 1997. 80-96.

Glazer, Miriyam. "Orphans of Culture and History: Gender and Spirituality in Contemporary Jewish-American Women's Novels." *Tulsa Studies in Women's Literature* 13.1 (Spring 1994): 127-41.

Glazer, Miriyam. "The Will to Be Known: An Introduction to Contemporary Jewish-American Women Writers." *Studies in American Jewish Literature* 11.2 (Fall 1992): 125-27.

Gold, Nora. *Marrow and Other Stories*. Toronto/Los Angeles: Warwick, 1998.

Goodman, Allegra. "Writing Jewish Fiction In and Out of the Multicultural Context." *Daughters of Valor: Contemporary Jewish American Women Writers*. Eds. Jay L. Halio and Ben Siegel. Newark: University of Delaware Press, 1997. 268-74.

Hoy, Nancy Jody. "Of Holy Writing and Priestly Voices: A Talk with Esther Broner." *Massachusetts Review* 24.2 (Summer 1983): 254-69.

Radway, Janice A. *Reading the Romance: Women, Patriarchy, and Popular Literature*. Chapel Hill: University of North Carolina Press, 1984.

Shapiro, Ann R. Introduction. *Jewish American Women Writers: A Bio-Bibliographical and Critical Sourcebook*. Eds. A. R. Shapiro, Sara R. Horowitz, Ellen Schiff, and Miriyam Glazer. Westport: Greenwood Press, 1994. 1-14.

# 5.
# From Complicity to Subversion

## The Female Subject in Adele Wiseman's Novels

An examination of the female subject in Adele Wiseman's novels charts the radical shift from complicity with the patriarchy of orthodox Judaism in *The Sacrifice* (1956) to subversion of that culture in *Crackpot* (1974). Both works describe insular communities whose ideologies, rather than their practices, reflect a traditional and orthodox Judaism and who participate minimally in the larger society. Each novel configures one female character as a "whore" who exists on the periphery of the community. *The Sacrifice* finally refuses to accommodate the prostitute. An example of "a female character who cannot properly negotiate an entrance into teleological love relations, ones with appropriate ends, a character whose marginalization grows concentrically as the novel moves to the end" (DuPlessis 16), Laiah is murdered for challenging Judaism's patriarchy. In the figure of Hoda, *Crackpot* seeks retribution for Laiah's death and provides a revisionist reading of the earlier text that attempts to recover a place for women within Judaism, and within fiction. As this essay will show, *Crackpot* is written against *The Sacrifice* as a critique where "community and social connectedness are the end of the female quest, not death" (DuPlessis 16).

Wiseman's first novel "sacrifices" a female sensibility to the patriarchal discourse of orthodox Judaism. Primarily a tragedy, *The Sacrifice* is a male-centred text whose prevailing consciousness is that of Abraham. Despite his slaying of Laiah, the narrator is aligned consistently with Abraham, an alliance that is signalled early on through a detailed description of his physical discomfort. As repeated references to his eyes suggest, Abraham's vision, however distorted, will dominate the work: "The train was beginning to slow down again, and Abraham noticed lights in the distance.... He tried to close his eyes and lose himself in the thick, dream-crowded stillness, but his eyelids, prickly with weariness, sprang open again" (3). By focusing on Abraham's singular perception and his decision to disembark the train, the narrator deliberately and immediately positions him at the centre of the action. Further, early references to his "throbbing aches" (3), flawed vision, and rash behaviour foreshadow the similar responses that overwhelm Abraham during his murder of Laiah.

That Abraham sanctions compliance for women is evident in his attitude toward Sarah, his wife, Ruth, his daughter-in-law, and Laiah, the local temptress who seeks his attention. In fact, in the world of *The Sacrifice*, if one is female acting is tantamount to sinning. Hence, Abraham endorses his wife's debilitating passivity as an appropriate response to the tragic loss of her elder sons without understanding that she is silenced by the cultural imperative to internalize her tremendous grief, manifested as "spasms" that only "wear themselves out in exhaustion" (50). Chaim Knopp and other male characters respect Sarah for her submissiveness. In defiance of his own loquacious wife, for example, Mr. Plopler wistfully describes Sarah as "such a quiet one" (134). The one time she differs with her husband by correcting his conscious misattribution of a Christian cousin to her side of the family, Sarah does so timorously, speaking softly with "her troubled gaze on her hands in front of her" (125). As her husband apologizes she looks down, feeling "ashamed of what she had let slip," and is soon "silent in his arms, as though already distant" (125). Sarah's death occurs in the following chapter, soon after her momentary transgression of the norms that govern female humility.

In contrast, Sonya Plopler and Bassieh Knopp have distinctive voices throughout the novel and continually announce their personal desires. Their direct manners and forthrightness, however, offend the other characters. Moreover, the narrator's endorsement of this distaste becomes evident in the comic moments that often are achieved at the expense of Sonya Plopler's penchant for gossip and Bassieh Knopp's tendency toward self-aggrandizement.

Despite her irritation with her mother-in-law, Ruth admires the marriage of Sarah and Abraham, the success of which depends on the rigid adherence to culturally sanctioned roles and their attendant codes of behaviour. Ruth aspires to a similar shared intimacy between herself and Isaac. Although she does not envisage herself as fragile, she fantasizes that Isaac may one day treat her "as though she were made of glass" (134). This reverie conforms to the values of orthodox Judaism upheld by Abraham. As long as Ruth cleaves to this fantasy she does not provoke her father-in-law. When she takes the initiative required to support herself and her family after Isaac's death, however, she challenges Abraham's ideal of the dependent and passive female.

Ruth's cataclysmic argument with Abraham is spurred by her decision to act, a move toward economic independence that is the catalyst for the murder of Laiah. Like Sarah, whose lifelong suffering is the aftermath of the irrational killing of her sons during a pogrom in Russia, Ruth bears the burden of another's crime. She continually fights "the impulse to blame herself" (310) for Abraham's murder of Laiah and is plagued by the fear that she has misunderstood her father-in-law. Powerless whether or not they embrace the subordinate position that Judaism traditionally assigns to women, the novel's female characters bear a weight of suffering.

Although Laiah shares in the suffering of Sarah and Ruth, her pain is heightened for she is denied the respect they receive as wives and mothers. Further, as a prostitute she is ostracized by the same women who otherwise would offer her community. Laiah therefore is marginalized by her marital status, by her childlessness, and by her livelihood. But marginalization proves insufficient punishment for Laiah's offences. Her deliberate challenging of Judaism, which deems it highly inappropriate for a woman to behave as temptress, cannot succeed within the world of *The Sacrifice*. As Nancy K. Miller states, "in so much women's fiction a world outside love proves to be out of the world altogether" (45). As a result, Laiah endures material and emotional hardship: economic insecurity, failed relationships, the denial of love and friendship, loneliness, verbal and sexual provocation, and barrenness. Her desire to give and receive love is repeatedly and sadly misinterpreted by a community that does not condone the expression of female desire, sexual or otherwise.

Unlike the characters in the novel, the narrator periodically shows sympathy for Laiah: "Life had not dealt squarely with her. Nothing had ever gone right for her from the very start" (192). More often, however, the narrator mirrors Abraham's dominant attitude toward Laiah and treats her with irony and disdain. Laiah is presented primarily as a hypocritical woman who yearns for acceptance by the same society whose patriarchal constraints she publicly defies with her displays of vanity, sensuality, and worldly knowledge.

The slaying of Laiah is meant to silence a woman who protests against the narrowness of her life as a Jewish woman and who seeks through self-expression and personal freedom to undermine Judaic convention. Rachel Blau DuPlessis explains:

> Death comes for a female character when she has a jumbled, distorted, inappropriate relation to the "social script" or plot designed to contain her legally, economically, and sexually. Death is the result when energies of selfhood, often represented by sexuality, at once their most enticing and most damaging expression, are expended outside the "couvert" of marriage or valid romance: through adultery … loss of virginity or even suspected "impurity" … or generalized female passion …. (15)

Laiah, who is described ironically as a "devil" (33), is guilty of all the above—adultery, impurity, and passion. Moreover, her sexual desire is couched in incestuous language: Abraham is confused by the "childish petulance in Laiah's voice" (302) when she asks, "'Little father' … 'will you be good to me?'" (300-301). Unlike the lesser transgressions of Sarah and Ruth, Laiah's transgressions are sexual in nature and therefore punishable. As DuPlessis affirms, "Death in general is a more than economic arrangement, for the punishment of one desire is the end of all" (16). In a scene that recalls Abraham's profane slaughter of a cow when he was apprenticed to a corrupt butcher, Laiah is attributed bovine features and is ceremoniously butchered: "under her eyelids her eyebulbs were large and fine. Her forehead wrinkled and was somehow sad, like that of some time-forgotten creature that had crept out to seek the sun" (303). Unlike his biblical namesake who is prevented from sacrificing Isaac, the fictional Abraham carries out the murder of Laiah.

Within this tradition-bound society the norms of patriarchy will not be flouted without repercussions and Laiah is killed for her indiscretion, a shocking articulation of the misogyny that is embedded in orthodox Judaism. In its denial of reconciliation and reparation to its female characters, privileges that the novel finally accords its male characters, *The Sacrifice* proclaims itself a patriarchal text.

In *Crackpot*, published eighteen years after *The Sacrifice*, the fate of the female subject is radically revised. While *The Sacrifice* draws to a close with Laiah's corpse and its flow of "warm blood" (304), *Crackpot* begins and concludes with large, accommodating, sensual Hoda. In Wiseman's second novel, a female-centred work written in the comic mode, the nurturing matriarch has displaced the overseer, judge, and patriarch of *The Sacrifice* and the narrator is aligned with the female rather than the male subject.

*Crackpot* prefers Hoda's physical ampleness and earthy appetite to Abraham's noble stature and his disavowal of pleasure. Hoda challenges her assigned passive role. Demanding to be seen and heard, she rejects the silence of Sarah in favour of garrulity and, unlike Ruth who toils respectably for years, Hoda achieves an economic success that exceeds her initial expectations. Moreover, unlike Laiah, Hoda publicly embraces her work. She is not alienated or punished or murdered for her choice of vocation; rather, she is rewarded with love and marriage. *Crackpot* is a novel of celebration, a record of the singular triumph of a Jewish prostitute.[1] Eighteen years earlier Laiah had been denied a similar success. By 1974, however, a different vision and a revised understanding of women's position within Judaism are articulated in *Crackpot* that, partly through mood and characterization, subverts orthodox tradition.

Whereas the first pages of *The Sacrifice* construct the male as the dominant subject and prevailing consciousness of the novel, *Crackpot* opens with an engaging description of Rahel and Hoda, her overfed daughter. The work immediately affirms the secondary position of its male characters in relation to their female counterparts and the dominance of the female voice. *Crackpot* redraws the family matrix to consist of a husband who is a passive idealist, a wife who is a wage-earner, and a child who is a self-willed individual. While Abraham remains the noble patriarch throughout the tragic turn of events in *The Sacrifice,* Danile, Hoda's father, never enjoys the position of a man who either is revered by the Jewish community or respected as the head of a household. Because of his blindness and inability to support his family, Danile is marginalized by his own people and is thus perceived as largely ineffectual as both husband and father. Danile's position within the community and his family is superseded by Rahel who, despite her own infirmity, supports her family by cleaning the homes of Jewish families and by Hoda who assumes responsibility for her father following Rahel's death, whose perspective dominates the work, and with whom the narrator is compassionately aligned. The sympathetic portrayal of Hoda contrasts sharply with the previously ironic treatment of Laiah. By the second paragraph of the novel, when the young Hoda rumbles "Maa-a-a-a-ah" in "a surprisingly chesty contralto" (7), she has laid claim to the text. The prostitute as enticer in *The Sacrifice* is recast in *Crackpot* as the prostitute-cum-earth mother who displaces the male in an affirming tale of "condoms," "prurience," and "incestry" (300).

Unlike *The Sacrifice,* where narrative irony connotes disdain and several characters express their disapproval of Laiah's sexuality, *Crackpot* conveys admiration for Hoda through comic irony. Hoda is respected for behaviour that challenges Judaism's ethos of female submissiveness, the same behaviour for which Laiah is vilified in *The Sacrifice.* At the Public Health Office, for example, where she is tested for venereal disease and all but proclaims herself a prostitute to the others seated in the waiting room, Hoda forfeits neither the narrator's nor the reader's approbation. Rather, she is described as having "developed, over the years, a kind of sophistication, a public attitude, a way of outfacing whoever faced her. Deliberately, she would introduce the question, 'What do you do for a living?' so that she could work round to telling them, in her turn, still sloshing her [urine] specimen innocently, 'Me? Oh, I make ends meet'" (210). In contrast to Laiah, whose several attempts to achieve self-sufficiency are thwarted, Hoda appears throughout *Crackpot* as she is described above: resourceful, independent, and heroic. The shift from tragedy in *The Sacrifice* to comedy in *Crackpot*,[2] which signals the move from solemnity to celebration and from a critical to a sympathetic narrator, indicates support for Hoda's challenging of normative behaviour for women and allows for her personal triumph at the close of the novel.

The marked similarities between Hoda and Laiah are their prostitution and the marginalized status attributed to them by others. The characterization of Hoda differs from that of Laiah, however, in significant ways. Rather than suffer for her choice of vocation, Hoda flourishes in spite of it. She successfully supports herself and her father with her meagre income. Hoda enjoys long-lasting relationships with friends and family members and strives to sustain difficult associations with her Uncle Nate, for example, among others. Unlike Laiah, whose family history is undisclosed, Hoda is the cherished daughter of devoted parents. Later, she nurtures her elderly father whose familial memories serve as her own lifeline. Hoda shares the companionship of her colleague, Seraphina, without the jealousy and competition that exists between Laiah and her friend, Jenny. Moreover, Hoda serves both the therapeutic and sexual needs of her customers, many of whom regard her as their friend.

Hoda refuses to be excluded and participates as a secular member of the Jewish community, as well as a citizen of the large urban centre in which she lives. Although she often feels alone and disconnected, hers is not a predominantly lonely life as is Laiah's. In contrast to Laiah, Hoda responds to verbal or sexual provocation with characteristic humour, a limited means of self-protection adopted by Jews throughout history. Solemn reactions are reserved for situations that warrant them, such as Hoda's first incestuous encounter with her son David. Moreover, unlike Laiah, Hoda bears a child who is both the cause of tremendous anguish and the vehicle for her personal reconciliation that concludes the novel.

In fact, it is primarily the act of childbirth that distinguishes Hoda from Laiah. Judaism views the birth of a son as a privilege and the birth of a male child confers high status on a woman.

Although she is denied that status by virtue of her occupation and her circumstances as an unwed mother, Hoda reclaims her son through incest.

In *The Sacrifice* the incestuous desire of Laiah for Abraham is metaphoric and implicit. In *Crackpot,* however, the act of incest is central and is both subversive and subverted by the novel. In a parodic inversion of mother-son incest, *Crackpot* turns the tale of Jocasta and Oedipus on its head. Instead of engendering tragedy and alienation as it does in the Theban drama, the incestuous relationship between Hoda and David facilitates the novel's comic resolution. As Linda Hutcheon explains, "Parody today is endowed with the power to renew. It need not do so, but it can.... What has traditionally been called parody privileges the normative impulse, but today's art abounds as well in examples of parody's power to revitalize" (115).

In another parody of the Old Testament story of Lot, Abraham's biblical nephew who remains unaware of his incestuous encounters with his daughters, Hoda assumes the unlikely position of maternal authority by displacing the father and choosing to accept her son as sexual partner. Here, incest is neither an unacknowledged act, as in the case of Jocasta and Oedipus, nor a means of begetting male heirs, as in the case of Lot and his daughters (Gen. 19:30-38).

Instead, incest becomes an act of compassion as Hoda selflessly enters a relationship with David who, like Oedipus and Lot, remains oblivious to the true nature of the sexual union in which he participates. Although Hoda suffers with the knowledge that she is David's mother, the decision to succumb to his request for sexual relations is prompted by maternal concern and she is careful not to abuse her position of power. Moreover, through their incestuous connection Hoda and David are united spiritually.

The use of incest as a means of achieving reconciliation subverts the general understanding of the act as one in which the father is the perpetrator of a sexual crime and the daughter is the violated innocent. The reversal of roles in *Crackpot* does not have devastating results, as incest usually does in fiction and reality. Instead, both female and male subjects mature as a result of their intimacy and move on to more gratifying experiences.

The engagement of Hoda and Lazar, with which the novel

concludes, is characteristic of the affirming nature of comedy. In contrast to Laiah, who is brutalized and silenced for her deviant behaviour, Hoda is rewarded with marriage through which she finally is reinscribed into Judaism. As she relinquishes her vocation and assumes the role "of a good wife" (298) she secures a place within her religion and her community. While marriage to Lazar and potential childbirth may suggest the objectification of Hoda through a loss of individuality and independence, an ending "in which the gain is both financial and romantic success in the 'heterosexual contract'" (DuPlessis 4), Hoda's reinscription into Judaism must be seen as a celebration of renewed opportunity, a revision of the unsatisfactory alternatives available to women in *The Sacrifice*.

Hoda is neither silenced nor destined to the solitary life of an aging prostitute; rather, she is allowed personal fulfillment, a subversive achievement for women, to say nothing of prostitutes, within Judaism. In her discovery that "she really liked love, now that she had found out exactly where it lived and how it worked. Love lived where it couldn't help itself, had to say yes, couldn't resist and had to give in, couldn't think, couldn't hide, couldn't pretend" (108), Hoda triumphs where Laiah is punished.

*The Sacrifice* and *Crackpot* construct a female subject as prostitute in order to free her from the limitations imposed on all women, married or single. While *The Sacrifice* does not embrace the prostitute, who already exists on the margins of society, and castigates her for desiring freedom, *Crackpot* celebrates her life and rewards her with integration. Whereas Laiah weakens over time, Hoda literally and figuratively proves larger than the constraints of the patriarchy. *Crackpot*'s revisionist reading of the earlier novel is an atonement for the unholy, parodic "sacrifice" of Laiah and an attempt to locate a place for women within Judaism and fiction which will foster their independence and accommodate rather than repress their individuality.

## Notes

[1]The figure of the Jewish prostitute is rare enough in Canadian literature. A third example occurs in Miriam Waddington's poem

"The Bond," where the speaker identifies herself with a "Whore, Jewess" who is "twice outcast" (9-10).

[2] Although the critical reevaluation of genre from a feminist perspective is relevant to my argument, I have refrained from a generic examination of Wiseman's novels since that is not the focus of this essay.

## Works Cited

DuPlessis, Rachel Blau. *Writing Beyond the Ending: Narrative Strategies of Twentieth-Century Women Writers*. Bloomington: Indiana University Press, 1985.

Hutcheon, Linda. *A Theory of Parody: The Teachings of Twentieth-Century Art Forms*. New York: Methuen, 1985.

Miller, Nancy K. *Subject to Change: Reading Feminist Writing*. New York: Columbia University Press, 1988.

*New English Bible*. Oxford: Oxford University Press, 1970.

Sophocles. "King Oedipus." *The Theban Plays*. By Sophocles. Trans. E. F. Watling. Markham, ON: Penguin, 1978.

Waddington, Miriam. "The Bond." *Collected Poems*. By M. Waddinton. Toronto: Oxford University Press, 1986. 9-10.

Wiseman, Adele. *Crackpot*. Toronto: McClelland and Stewart, 1974.

Wiseman, Adele. *The Sacrifice*. Toronto: Macmillan, 1956.

# 6.
# "This Was Her Punishment"

Jew, Whore, Mother in the Fiction of Adele Wiseman and Lilian Nattel

Miriam Waddington's 1942 poem "The Bond" characterizes a "Jewish whore" as "twice outcast" (9), "twice isolate" (10). As "Jewess" (10) and as whore, the woman who forms the locus of Waddington's poem is positioned at the margins of Canadian society. Ostracized for being a Jew—she experiences anti-Semitism on Toronto's Jarvis Street where she works during the 1940s—she is condemned to further isolation for her crime of prostitution and suffers alienation. In fact, as historian of medicine Lara Marks confirms, the Jewish prostitute faced "a triple oppression—as a woman, as a Jew and as a member of the Jewish working-class" ("Jewish" 7)—and she "symbolized the tenuous position and vulnerability of Jewish women as a whole" (10). A rare enough figure in Canadian literature, the Jewish prostitute reappears in the fiction of Adele Wiseman and Lilian Nattel, with an important difference: she is also a mother. Through a study of two novels, Wiseman's *Crackpot* (1974) and Nattel's *The Singing Fire* (2004), this essay considers the punishing cost to Jewish prostitutes who dare to become mothers. In charting the course of maternal suffering in novels by Adele Wiseman and Lilian Nattel, this essay shows the Jewish whore/mother as a figure thrice outcast, thrice isolate.

In Wiseman's comic novel, the protagonist Hoda is an obese Jewish prostitute who services the boys and men of her North Winnipeg community. When she becomes pregnant, Hoda labours alone, delivers her son in the isolation of her bedroom, and severs the umbilical cord that joins mother and baby. She soon realizes, however, that caring for a newborn will prevent her from earning a living to support herself and her blind father. Against her will, Hoda leaves her infant son in the care of the local orphanage, only to reencounter him years later when, as an adolescent, he presents himself as a client. When Nehama Korzen arrives from Plotsk, Poland in 1875, Nattel's protagonist immediately is trapped within the corrupt and fetid streets of London's East End and forced into a life of prostitution. Following a brutal beating by her pimp, she suffers a miscarriage and is close to death. For her illicit behaviour, Nehama is punished with infertility and is unable to bear a child in marriage. Although she yearns for a child of her own, she must be satisfied as an adoptive mother to a daughter who, as a teenager, is also lured to prostitution.

In configuring their protagonists as mothers, Wiseman and Nattel may appear to be subverting the conventional view of the prostitute as amoral and antisocial, as well as the traditional notion of the Jewish mother as proper upholder "of the family's morality and respectability" (Marks, "Jewish" 9) and as guardian of the community. Neither novel, however, sanctions the Jewish prostitute/mother. Denied maternal protection, neither Hoda nor Nehama enters prostitution knowingly, for example. Further, each woman is made into an aberrant mother of a child who is tainted at birth. Finally, that neither Hoda nor Nehama remains a prostitute suggests that prostitution and mothering are irreconcilable; in fact, the Jewish prostitute must be made to suffer in extraordinary ways for her trespass into motherhood.

Despite the persistent and widespread belief that prostitution within the Jewish community "was always insignificant" (Marks, "Jewish" 6), historical and literary evidence suggest otherwise. Scholarly studies, government documents, and archival records confirm the presence of Jewish prostitutes in urban centres such as Warsaw, London, Buenos Aires, New York, and Montreal, for example.[1] Maimie Pinzer (1885-?), who worked as a prostitute in Philadelphia in the early years of the twentieth century, left a remarkable record of her life in voluminous letters written between 1910 and 1922 to her benefactor, Fanny Quincy Howe (1870-1933), a wealthy Bostonian. At the request of Philadelphia social worker Herbert Welsh, who sought to prevent Pinzer's return to prostitution after she had lost her left eye, "possibly to syphilitic infection" (Rosen xiv), Howe initiated a correspondence that would foster a deep friendship between herself and Pinzer, women of vastly dissimilar backgrounds. In a correspondence housed at the Schlesinger Library of the Radcliffe Institute, and published as a selected edition in 1997, Pinzer articulates the vulnerable and pitiable position of the contemporary prostitute in a society that regarded her as foul and dispensable.

More pertinent to the focus of this essay, however, are the maternal experiences and feelings Pinzer describes throughout her correspondence. Repeatedly, Pinzer shows herself to be as much nurturer as former prostitute. She claims, for example, that she "really can do almost any work that a child's nurse does, for I have helped so often with them" (20), and her letters show this to be the case. She is "in the room" (49) when her sister-in-law Caroline gives birth in 1911, and she helps care for her infant niece Sarah, even as she writes to Howe—"I have the baby on my lap and she seems quiet, [content] just to watch the pen bob about, since it is a red pen-holder and attracts her eye" (99). She attends to the baby's daily needs, often sleeps with her, and regularly brings her gifts. When she has to assist in her brother's grocery store, Pinzer cannot bear leaving her charge: "I love her so much that it is hard to be away from her all day. She's so heavy now that it leaves me all worn out to frolic with her, and yet I can't resist her" (113). Later, when a rift with her brother prevents Pinzer from seeing Sarah, she feels "forced to drive the baby out of my thoughts and heart; otherwise, I should be very miserable when I think of her" (135).

In 1918, Pinzer successfully nursed her niece through an influenza pandemic that swept the United States. When her sister-in-law succumbed to the disease, she adopted Sarah and younger brother David and raised them with her husband, Ira Benjamin, whom she had known since adolescence and married in January 1917. Pinzer herself likely suffered a miscarriage in 1917, a loss she must have felt keenly, for she understood the depth of maternal love. When her sister-in-law died, she wrote openly to Howe:

> When I lost my baby last year, Caroline, who wrote to me secretly (for [my brother] James had forbidden it), said

she felt so badly for me, that if she were able, she'd send Sarah to me to stay for awhile to comfort me. I can recall now that I thought that I'd rather have Potsy [i.e. Sarah] than even my own baby. And now I have her, and I love her, but how it hurts me; for she loved her mother, and it is so sad for her. (413-14)

The portrait of Maimie Pinzer that emerges from her letters, acclaimed for their historical and literary value, serves to counter the general perception of prostitutes as hardened individuals, incapable of love, and especially ill-fitted to become mothers. Her honesty, emotional intensity, and maternal desire echo through the fictional lives of Hoda and Nehama. Along with Pinzer, who nurtured two adopted children but would neither bear nor raise her own child, they, too, suffer in motherhood.

Like Pinzer, Hoda and Nehama "fall" into prostitution. Following the murder of her father when she was thirteen, Pinzer was forced to leave secondary school and seek employment as a department store clerk. Her small earnings helped support her family, including her verbally abusive mother and sexually abusive uncle. Unable, however, to abide the pain of living at home and the restrictions imposed by her mother, Pinzer began to date boys. She was arrested upon a complaint made by her mother and uncle, imprisoned, and then sent for a year to Magdalen Home for Wayward Girls. When she was released in 1899, Pinzer and her lover Frank Sloan fled to Boston. For four years, between the ages of fourteen and eighteen, Pinzer lived and worked in Boston as an actor at Columbia Theatre, a "nude model for art classes," and a prostitute (Rosen xxii).

As Marks explains, "exclusion from both the host society and the Jewish community [often] left women with little alternative but to turn to prostitution to support themselves" ("Jewish" 9). Hoda, like Pinzer, begins her life as a prostitute following the early death of a parent. When her humpbacked mother dies—Rahel's domestic work provided the family's sole income—Hoda is bereft of maternal guidance and family support. Her great-uncle Nate, who had sponsored Hoda and her parents and had paid for their voyage from Russia to North America, suggests that Hoda be sent to the Jewish Children's Orphanage and her father, Danile, to the Jewish Old People's Home. Unwilling to accept her uncle's selfish plans, the adolescent Hoda is left alone to care for her blind father. That she succeeds in doing so shows her youthful determination and resourcefulness as a prostitute in the face of ostracism.

The comic mode of Wiseman's novel, particularly its humorous scenes and affirming close, may leaven one's reading of *Crackpot*, but it does not soften Hoda's humiliating entry into prostitution and the exploitation she experiences. A childhood game of "Doctors and Nurses" (30) leads Hoda to seek out the "bad company" (93) of boys and men. Soon, she is masturbating Yankl the butcher in exchange for "meat scraps" (80) necessary for dinner. While cleaning the Pankess home, her late mother's customer, she receives a dime from Mr. Pankess when he fondles her buttocks. Hoda communes with boys, enjoys their rough language and play, but she quickly becomes a sexual target for adolescent males. After she gives in to her own sexual desire and that of her schoolmate Morgan, who wins the right to seduce Hoda in a betting match, she feels "let down," "uncomfortable," and "unclean," although she cannot remember the "reasons why she felt awful, and she didn't even know how far it was her own fault" (109). Hoda is ambivalent: she feels guilty for having sex but concedes that Morgan had made "her feel so good" (110).

Faced, however, with the pressing need to sustain herself and her father, Hoda is less moral than practical and reasons that "the money Morgan had given her [from his winnings] ... was another good thing. She and Daddy could use that all right" (109). When she learns that sex can be profitable, Hoda sheds her innocence among boys, but not her amiability, and determines "to work up a source of steadier income, so as not to have to rely on one person's whims for hers and her daddy's well-being" (121). She easily convinces her innocent father that she is helping students with their school work, sets up shop in her bedroom, and is soon servicing the boys of her vicinity. With her livelihood ensured, Hoda quickly abandons any lingering sense of guilt. As a moral being for whom the child-parent bond is paramount, however, she regrets having to deceive her father.

Despite her sexual precociousness, Hoda remains emotionally

innocent for she does not venture beyond the familiar boundaries of her home and her neighbourhood. The one time she travels downtown with her friend Seraphina to work at a dance hall, she is nearly raped by a hostile client. Hoda prefers the regular work available locally, at weddings, for example, where middle-aged men pay the "poor orphan, at times with an unexpected generosity born of schnapps and gratitude and the rare surprise of it all" (129), for their furtive sexual encounters in alleys, boiler rooms, against trees or walls. Hoda's presence at communal events is soon expected, in fact, and her role within the Jewish community accepted. Marks cites "many examples of Jewish prostitutes being accepted as part of a 'natural' way of life. While the middle-class, older, established Jews bitterly criticized it, the newcomers, who were mostly working-class and facing poverty, had much more sympathy with it and could understand the reasons women went into [prostitution]" ("Jewish" 9-10). The fictional community that embraced Hoda—although unnamed, it resembles the North End of Winnipeg of the 1930s and 1940s where Wiseman was raised—was comprised largely of immigrants concerned more with day-to-day survival than the moral issues surrounding prostitution. Eventually, Hoda becomes "something of a legend in the district, as the girl who had broken in just about every mother's son of them" (144).

Although she is less ostracized in fiction than Maimie Pinzer was in life, Hoda feels isolated, without "a real friend" (140). She is physically intimate with boys and men, but Hoda remains outside the community of women. She lacks girlfriends and her mother dies before she could "answer the [pressing] questions" (140) Hoda increasingly ponders. She assumes she is "pretty safe the way she operated because when you went out with a lot of guys it was more like scrambling the parts of a whole bunch of jig-saw puzzles" (141), but Hoda is not confident that she knows all that is necessary to avoid becoming pregnant, for example. Like Pinzer, who was rejected by her mother, Hoda lacks maternal affection and protection. As women alone, Pinzer and Hoda are especially vulnerable to misinformation, illness, and violence. As prostitutes, however, they are seen by their own communities as deserving of suffering.

Hoda's suffering is extreme when she becomes a mother. Although her aberrant work as a prostitute is condoned by the community, when she gives birth to a son, albeit unknowingly, she commits an unsanctioned moral trespass. The prostitute is tolerated as long as she serves the sexual needs of men. When she dares to become a mother and thereby an agent who must act independently, in the interests of herself and her child, she defies communal standards for sex workers. Hoda pays dearly for that defiance—she must give up her child and suffer emotional trauma—for neither fiction nor life will accommodate the prostitute/mother.

Hoda's ignorance and her obesity mask her pregnancy. Thus, when she goes into labour she thinks "the sudden, atrocious pain" (153) is a severe stomach cramp and only realizes that she has delivered an infant when the slimy lump on her bed squirms and squawks. Having given birth in the middle of the night, while her father sleeps in the next room, Hoda grows frantic with anxiety. Terrified that Danile will waken to the baby's cries and discover the truth about his daughter, Hoda takes decisive action. After she washes and swaddles her newborn, she deposits him on the steps of the Jewish orphanage where he is found and subsequently raised to adolescence under the particular care of the director's wife. The boy is doubly tainted by his illegitimate birth and a protruding navel, a disfigurement that results from his mother's clumsy severing and double knotting of the umbilical cord. In fact, the moment of birth remains indelibly imprinted on both son and mother, whose private burden of "memory of her black night" (170) and irreconcilable guilt are felt as regular assaults of "almost superstitious fear" and "acute panic" (188).

At the moment of delivery Hoda understands that to keep her son would have a devastating impact on the child, herself, and her father. First, as the illegitimate child of a prostitute, the boy would lack any status in the community. Further, Hoda's status as mother would negatively affect her ability to work freely as a prostitute to support herself and her family. Moreover, she might risk rejection by her beloved father. In fact, many unmarried mothers, a large number of whom were prostitutes, "found it difficult [if not impossible] to keep their infants. … [U]nmarried mothers were not encouraged to take on the role of 'caring mother'.

Rather, motherhood was promoted as a responsibility which would remind unmarried mothers not to fall again" (Marks, "Luckless" 130-31). Indeed, Hoda learns from experience and becomes a responsible sex worker. Following the birth of her son, she acquires the knowledge she previously lacked and learns "how babies are made." She begins to use birth control and is examined regularly for sexually transmitted infections. Over time, she even comes "to accept the idea, particularly in relation to herself, that there were some things that she might not ever be able to make good" (221).

But to atone for her unnatural crime of becoming a mother, the prostitute must be made to suffer in extraordinary ways. Remorse and reform do not prevent the extreme pain that is finally meted out to Hoda in punishment for her "enormous, inerasable debt" (252). When her adolescent son presents himself as a client, Hoda, who recognizes him by his navel, must accept him. For her trespass into motherhood, she must become the incestuous prostitute/mother who initiates her son into sex. Here, incest becomes an unusually moral act that Hoda undertakes to protect her son; it is an act of atonement for the prostitute's crime of bearing a child; it is also an act that leads Hoda to "the outermost boundary of aloneness that can be reached by a human being" (256).

During the brief interval that her son becomes a regular client, Hoda never reveals her true identity as his mother. Rather, as a prostitute she comforts him, converses with him, and eases his difficult entry into adulthood. Hoda's extended sexual relationship with her son serves to prolong her private suffering, but it also affords the reconciliation of "all the aching fragments" (258) of her life. In fiction, as in life, the moral impropriety of the prostitute who becomes a mother, willingly or not, appears to justify her extreme punishment. That the prostitute/mother must be redeemed through excessive anguish attests to the heinousness of her crime and corroborates Adrienne Rich's assertion that women, who "have always been outside the (manmade) law ... have been much more stringently punished than men for breaking the law, as in the case of prostitution" (270).

Gradually, Hoda is released from suffering, but only after she ceases to work as a prostitute. When she accepts the job of hostess at a delicatessen, owned by a former client, she is able to relinquish sex work as a means of economic support. Still at the centre of her community as the doyenne of Limpy Letz's eating and gambling establishment, Hoda acquires a respectability she never knew as the local whore. She also acquires a suitor who seeks her hand in marriage. Through Lazar, a Holocaust survivor who literally crawled out of an open grave and over the corpses of his wife and children to claim his own life, Hoda is offered final redemption. By the close of *Crackpot*, in fact, both Hoda and Lazar are given new opportunities: she through her work in the delicatessen, he as a survivor who is determined to make a new life for himself in North America. But it is Hoda who is truly made anew. No longer a prostitute, she is a restaurant hostess. No longer alone, she will soon become Lazar's wife. Most significant, however, is Hoda's closing dream in which she is "*Almost a real mother!*" (304). Newly virginal as fiancée to Lazar, the promise of "true" motherhood is finally held out to the former prostitute who, the novel implies, may still bear a child in marriage.

Fresh opportunities and the offer of renewed life may be read as hard-won rewards for Hoda's suffering as a prostitute. They also suggest the absolute incompatibility of prostitution and mothering, however; for Hoda must relinquish her prior life as a prostitute—the triumphs and trials of her past, and especially the connection with her son—before she may enter marriage with its prospect of "real" motherhood. That she must do so confirms that legitimate motherhood is not available to the prostitute who will always remain alone, marginalized by the Jewish community she serves. Only a radical transformation—the prostitute turned virginal bride—allows for Hoda's communal reintegration.

In *The Singing Fire*, Nehama Korzen arrives in London from Plotsk in the late nineteenth century, a time when Jewish women, who settled in the crowded and impoverished East End of the city where the sex trade was firmly established, "were being cursed for prostitution ... [and] the Jewish prostitute symbolized the social evils which were undermining the strength of the family and the empire" (Marks, "Model" 3). Seeking to avoid an arranged marriage and a traditional life as Jewish wife and mother, the seventeen-year-old Nehama plans her escape. From her older sisters she steals a pair of earrings, a silk kerchief, and a blouse, sells the valuable items, and defies her parents by purchasing a ticket for London and fleeing her *shtetl* in Poland. When she lands on foreign soil, Nehama, like Maimie Pinzer and Hoda, lacks the parental protection, worldly knowledge, and experience that could prevent her "fall" into prostitution. Rather, as she sits alone in the fog of St. Katherine's dock, Nehama "prayed to God, Help me please, because that is what a person does when there is no one else" (7). When her prayers are answered in Yiddish by Mr. Blink, a portly, congenial man who claims to be a fellow Jew, she cannot know that he would soon deliver her to a brutal pimp.

Unlike Pinzer and Hoda, however, Nehama's entry into prostitution is not gradual. As a young woman travelling alone in 1875, Nehama is taken for a whore. Upon her arrival in London, she falls prey to Blink, a pimp's scout. The next morning, Blink bribes a constable to escort Nehama to the London Hospital, where she undergoes an internal examination for venereal infection. Under the Contagious Diseases Acts of 1864, 1866, and 1869, "designed to eliminate venereal disease" (Marks, "Jewish" 6), British police were permitted by law to detain and examine any woman they suspected of prostitution. That the virginal Nehama feels defiled by the physical examination is precisely the result Blink seeks as he intones, "So you're no longer a good girl" (20). Her defences already weakened, she is unprepared for her sadistic deflowering with a broom handle that is subsequently orchestrated by the Squire, the pimp who intends to ready her for work as a prostitute. Hence, within two days of her arrival, having been beaten into submission by physical brutality and private shame, Nehama yields to the will of her pimp and enters "the trade" (40).

A naive adolescent, Nehama accepts that she must work to repay the Squire's initial outlay of a ten-pound "entrance fee" (41) that admitted her to Britain. Increasingly dehumanized by the bleak circumstances of her life as an East End prostitute, Nehama grows convinced that "God ... [had] abandoned her to the evil inclination" (34). When she learns that she has been deceived, however, and that she is pregnant, she acts with the same agency that drove her flight from Poland and decides to escape to save herself and her baby. Like Pinzer and Hoda, Nehama is as much nurturer as whore. She sends loving letters to family members in Poland, for example, written to convince them that she is well and happy. She is protective of Sally, a much younger prostitute who is ill, even after Sally betrays Nehama's trust. Moreover, Nehama imagines a redemptive birth—she hopes to give birth "by the sea" to a baby with "fair hair" (45)—that will assuage her pain and heal her soul. She yearns for "her old life" (49) of hope, but Nehama's rescue will come at a tremendous cost.

Although she works among women, Nehama cannot rely on their friendship. When another woman reports her escape, Nehama's fate is sealed. Ironically, a niece's loyalty to her pimp uncle—the perverse result of extreme victimization—leads to Nehama's final release from prostitution, but not before she sustains permanent trauma. Following a brutal beating and knifing by the Squire, Nehama suffers a miscarriage, the nadir of her young life. Close to death, she recognizes that she lives within "a block" (49) of Jewish shops, and that if she were to "die in a Jewish street, maybe someone would say the prayer for the dead" (50). Drained and bleeding, Nehama drags herself to salvation in London's teeming Frying Pan Alley, the heart of the Jewish district.

Like Hoda, Nehama must flee the whorehouse before she is offered succour and companionship. Rescued from the street by Minnie, a kind passerby who intuits her plight, Nehama is afforded refuge when she is most vulnerable. As she recuperates in Minnie's home, where she mourns the loss of a child conceived out of the hardship of the recent past, she rediscovers her community, as well as her considerable talent as a seamstress. Having rejected the aberrant life of the prostitute, Nehama is proffered gentleness, but privately she remains "in exile," dreaming nightly "of a baby in a white cap trimmed with lace" (62). Although her life as a prostitute was foreshortened by a miscarriage, the pain Nehama endures as a result of her brief trespass into motherhood is no less extreme than the suffering of either Pinzer or Hoda. For her illicit behaviour, she, too, is denied the nurturing balm of motherhood that might salve her emotional and physical wounds.

Through Minnie and her husband Lazar, Nehama meets the man who becomes her husband. Nathan's love for Nehama is purifying;

when they make love on Sabbath afternoons, "he traced the scar on her thigh as if it didn't ruin the smoothness of her leg" (86), and when she becomes pregnant with Nathan's child, she once again envisages redemption: "The first one she miscarried didn't count. That was in another life. This baby was her husband's, her beloved's ... and she awaited their child, her heart heavy with joy" (88). In her late twenties, after she has long ceased to be a prostitute, Nehama enters marriage and anticipates legitimate motherhood. But as a former prostitute who dared to become pregnant, she bears an indelible stain that will bar her from bearing a child. When Nehama feels "a familiar pain in her belly," she understands that she is miscarrying for a second time and accepts "her punishment" (20): she "wasn't made right" and "there won't be any more" (89) babies. That Nathan's "child had run away from her womb" (90) is evidence of the taint that marks the prostitute/mother. Although she is granted safe haven with Nathan, Nehama must suffer the pain of barrenness.

The trauma of a second miscarriage leads Nehama back to St. Katharine's dock. There she rescues a solitary traveller—Emilia Rosenberg reminds Nehama of her younger self—from a pimp "who called out in a familiar language, his face full of concern" (93). Having been seduced and later abandoned by a young suitor, Emilia has forsaken her village in Poland for London. As Marks notes, "Unmarried mothers were known to leave home in order to conceal their pregnancy; [and] some of them came from ... Eastern Europe to England to bear their child" ("Luckless" 123). Unlike prostitutes, however, unmarried mothers were "[s]een as redeemable ... [and] occupied a higher position in the hierarchy of fallen women" ("Luckless" 127). When she offers the young woman a place to stay and learns that she is pregnant, Nehama becomes Emilia's protector. Bound to Emilia as Minnie was once bound to her, Nehama recognizes a unique opportunity to redress the pain of her own past by assisting Emilia through her pregnancy and caring for her newborn daughter. Ironically, it is Emilia, rather than Nathan, who gives Nehama what she most desires: the chance to be a mother.

When Emilia gives birth, she feels no connection to her daughter and abandons the one-week-old infant, leaving behind the cryptic note, "Nehama, please take her" (133). Rather than deliver her to the Jews' Orphan Asylum, Nehama decides to keep the baby. Marks confirms that "[n]eighbours ... who had some understanding of the desperate plight faced by an unmarried mother sometimes adopted ... illegitimate children" ("Luckless" 122). In fact, Nehama's neighbourly act benefits herself and Nathan, as well as Emilia and her abandoned daughter. Moreover, by accepting Emilia's baby as her own, Nehama initiates a healing process that would prove long and difficult, as she herself intuits: "Everything had worked out; she had a husband, she had a child, she had a means to earn a living. So why couldn't she sleep at night?" (139).

As an adoptive mother who is determined "to make a life" (227) for her daughter, Nehama faces extraordinary challenges that eventually lead to her redemption. When Nathan's right hand is severed in a cart accident and he can no longer work as a tailor, she rallies, helps dispel his depression, and encourages him to become a coffee vendor. Following a burglary in the family tailoring shop, Nehama manages to reestablish her business. It is her daughter Gittel, however, who tests Nehama's determination and will to survive.

An adolescent fantasy that her birth mother "was no good and somehow Gittel would make up for it" (318) lures the girl to Dorset Street, the haunt of pimps and whores, where Nehama must face her own past to save her daughter's future. Like Hoda, who is forced to confront the past when her son presents himself as a client, Nehama must follow her daughter's lead and return to the pub where the Squire still presides over his whores. There, she and Nathan find Gittel entertaining the elderly pimp by singing atop a table. When Nathan intervenes between Nehama and the Squire, who recognizes her as one of his former prostitutes, Gittel is saved.

Through the dramatic rescue of Gittel, each family member is healed. First, in the pub, where he finally discerns that his wife was once a prostitute, Nathan asserts, "Never mind. Just remember, where you go, I go" (308). Nathan's generous spirit and understanding brings new intimacy and trust to the bond he shares with his wife. Second, when she is reassured that her birth mother was not a prostitute for having borne an illegitimate child, Gittel feels newly bound to Nehama and "held on to Mama's hand" (317). Absolved of guilt, which she is too young to fully comprehend, Gittel is returned safely to the protection of family. Finally, Nehama's fear of the Squire, which has terrorized her for years, is dispelled through the brave encounter with her past. In returning to Dorset Street, she effectively reclaims her past and rescues her daughter's future. Moreover, Nehama's daring fosters a new honesty between herself and Nathan, and between herself and Gittel. Having freed her daughter from the tantalizing grip of the same pimp who once commanded Nehama's life, she recognizes that "Gittel was truly hers" (108) and finally feels herself to be a "true" mother. As she proclaims, "You think I wouldn't come to find you, my Gittel-Sarah? If someone tried to hurt you, I would kill him. I would lie down in the gutter and let anyone walk on my back to keep you safe, my daughter. Even from the next world, you can't lose me. I promise you" (316).

But in the end, despite her strength of character, Nehama does not warrant the same grace accorded Emilia, her former charge. As an unmarried mother, Emilia enjoys full redemption: having rejected her past, she succeeds in establishing a new life for herself, marries well, and is pregnant with her husband's child. When she flees the teeming East End, Emilia finds employment in a respectable department store. There she meets the affluent Jacob Zalkind who soon becomes her husband. Jacob's devotion to Emilia is complete: he is attentive and respectful, offers her unconditional love, and looks forward to raising their family together. Like Nathan whose affection for Nehama is unwavering, Jacob has an expansive capacity for love and, as the ending implies, forgives Emilia her past deceits.

Emilia, an unmarried mother, may be rehabilitated to new status within her community. In contrast to Emilia are Nehama, Hoda, and Maimie Pinzer, former prostitutes who once trespassed into motherhood and can never relinquish the hold of the past. In fact, neither fiction nor life will accommodate the prostitute/mother whose redemption is tempered by excessive suffering. The prostitute may reclaim her Jewish identity through marriage, but the right to legitimate motherhood will elude the Jewish prostitute who remains thrice outcast, thrice isolate from the community of Jews, women, and mothers that will neither forget nor forgive her improprieties.

**Notes**

[1] See, for example, Bristow; Gartner; and Vincent.

**Works Cited**

Bristow, Edward J. *Prostitution and Prejudice: The Jewish Fight Against White Slavery, 1870-1939*. Oxford: Clarendon Press, 1982.

Gartner, L. P. "Anglo-Jewry and the Jewish International Traffic in Prostitution, 1885-1914." *American Jewish Studies Review* 7-8 (1982-83): 129-78.

Marks, Lara. "Jewish Women and Jewish Prostitution in the East End of London." *Jewish Quarterly* 34.2 (1987): 6-10.

Marks, Lara. "'The Luckless Waifs and Strays of Humanity': Irish and Jewish Immigrant Unwed Mothers in London, 1870-1939." *Twentieth Century British History* 3.2 (1992): 113-37.

Marks, Lara. *Model Mothers: Jewish Mothers and Maternity Provision in East London, 1870-1939*. Oxford: Clarendon Press, 1994.

Nattel, Lilian. *The Singing Fire*. Toronto: Alfred A. Knopf Canada, 2004.

Pinzer, Maimie. *The Maimie Papers: Letters from an Ex-Prostitute*. New York: Feminist Press, 1997.

Rich, Adrienne. *Of Woman Born: Motherhood as Experience and Institution*. 1976. New York: W. W. Norton, 1995.

Rosen, Ruth. Introduction. *The Maimie Papers: Letters from an Ex-Prostitute*. By Maimie Pinzer. New York: Feminist Press, 1997. xiii-xliv.

Vincent, Isabel. *Bodies and Souls: The Tragic Plight of Three Jewish Women Forced into Prostitution in the Americas*. Toronto: Random House Canada, 2005.

Waddington, Miriam. "The Bond." *Collected Poems*. By M. Waddington. Toronto: Oxford University Press, 1986. 9-10.

Wiseman, Adele. *Crackpot*. Toronto: McClelland and Stewart, 1974.

# 7.
# "The Freedom to Write"

## The Memoirs of Fredelle Bruser Maynard and Joyce Maynard

> The classic mentor narrative is hierarchical. This, as should be obvious, is a masculine narrative.... Recently, however, other models, other stories have emerged, in part because of the emergence of women's stories of mentorship, sometimes less fraught with the psychological complexities, the Oedipal complexities of male mentor narratives, sometimes not.
> —David Lazar (25)

This essay examines the connection between mothering and mentoring in the work of writers Fredelle Bruser Maynard and her daughter Joyce Maynard and argues, with Adrienne Rich, that "[f]ew women growing up in patriarchal society can feel mothered enough; the power of our mothers, whatever their love for us and their struggles on our behalf, is too restricted" (243). Not surprisingly, there are few examples of mothers and daughters who have shared the vocation of writing.[1] Moreover, there are fewer instances when mothers and daughters have made public—through writing—their personal relationships. The complex and dynamic bond between Fredelle Bruser Maynard and Joyce Maynard[2] can be studied through their respective memoirs. Fredelle is author of *Raisins and Almonds* (1972) and *The Tree of Life* (1988). Her first volume, published when her daughters were already young adults, remains strikingly mute on the experience of motherhood. Only after a space of sixteen years, once they had become mothers themselves and were established in their respective careers, could Fredelle write frankly of herself as "a most imperfect mother"

(*Tree* 237) to daughters Rona[3] and Joyce. Joyce is author of a number of works in which she reflects on her relationship with her parents. I am concerned chiefly with her memoir *At Home in the World* (1998), which obviously has led to the title of this book. Here, Joyce writes with a new, self-proclaimed honesty of the mother who "put the pen in my hand" (ix), whose drive and ambition made her into the writer she has become. Fredelle, a non-traditional Jewish mother who followed the example of her own mother, educated her daughter and launched her career. In so doing, she chose mentoring over faith and culture as the primary means to nurture Joyce and prepare her for adulthood.

Many readers will recognize Joyce Maynard as the American teenager who in 1972 published an article in the *New York Times Magazine* entitled "An 18-Year-Old Looks Back on Life" (23 April). From that auspicious beginning, Joyce went on to a career as writer and journalist.[4] Upon publication, the media made much of *At Home in the World* for its graphic description of Joyce's brief and youthful liaison with the famously reclusive novelist J. D. Salinger. While some may be titillated by Joyce's rendering of a relationship doomed to failure from the beginning, I read her memoir for what it tells of a fraught love for her mother and a unique literary apprenticeship. In all likelihood—and despite her own career as journalist (print and television) and author of books on child-rearing[5]—Fredelle Bruser Maynard will be less familiar to readers than her famous daughter. By nature less of an exhibitionist than Joyce, Fredelle was less prolific and more discreet when writing of family relationships.

In this essay, I probe the problematic connection between two women, one of whom is mother and educator while the other is daughter and student. Even when the daughter enjoys maternal protection—as in the case of Joyce, whose situation differs from most female protagonists discussed in this volume—an unresolved tension is palpable in the public writing of daughter and mother. Joyce values the skills her mother taught her, making her a precocious intellectual, while Fredelle encourages the dependence and love of her younger daughter. But a close study of the intimate revelations offered in their respective memoirs points to a strain between daughter and mother, the result of a blending of roles.

The education of a daughter always is rife with difficulty, even more so when the mother hopes to educate her child in ways that will ensure her independence of mind and ability to earn a living. Joyce appreciates and practices the writing her mother so deliberately taught her, but she always yearns for more. This is perhaps an example of "double vision" as Rich describes the "girl-child" who, despite a true and irreplaceable connection between herself and her mother, longs "for a woman's nurture, tenderness, and approval, a woman's power exerted in our defense, a woman's smell and touch and voice, a woman's strong arms around us in moments of fear and pain" (224). The remarkable relationship between Fredelle and Joyce—possibly unique among female writers—reveals the personal cost to both parent and child when mother chooses to educate her daughter to compete and succeed "in the world."

In this reading of the memoirs of Fredelle Bruser Maynard and Joyce Maynard I do not mean to conflate writerly selves with the actual women. Fredelle who speaks out from the pages of *The Tree of Life* and Joyce who narrates her personal journey in *At Home in the World* are separate from the real Fredelle and Joyce, writerly constructs that bear resemblance to their actual creators but remain apart from them at the same time. This essay focuses on the public record—available in each writer's memoir—of otherwise private relationships.

Toward the end of *The Tree of Life*, Fredelle admits "I wanted my daughters to be successful writers and—successfully, but at some cost—pushed them towards that goal" (241). Indeed, fearing her daughters' failures would become her own (*Tree* 241), Fredelle was, by her own admission, a strict taskmaster: "When I was a young mother, I knew all about the dangers of spoiling a child.... So I made, and tried to keep, a lot of rules. I ran a tight ship" (*Tree* 241). Early in her own memoir, Joyce corroborates this image of a mother who carefully coached her children to write: "Before we knew how to form alphabet letters ourselves, we gave dictation. We spoke; our mother wrote down what we said and told us how to make it better. Soon enough, she gave us a typewriter" (*At Home* 39).

Parent and child understood early on that their relationship combined traditional nurturing with practical mentoring. While she attended to her daughter's physical and emotional needs, Fredelle fostered a facility with language that could lead Joyce to a career as writer. Fredelle's overweening desire for her daughter's success was rooted partly in professional and personal frustration. As Rishma Dunlop has noted, "The roles of intellectual women have an uneasy history, played out against prescribed social relations. For women committed to intellectual work, achieving coherence with their social lives is difficult and contradictory" (115). Despite her own brilliance—she earned a Ph.D. from Radcliffe and graduated summa cum laude—Fredelle was refused a position in the Department of English at the University of New Hampshire, where her husband taught. In the 1950s, the University's strict policy against hiring faculty wives launched Fredelle on her successful career as writer and journalist. Throughout her life, however, she railed against the academic hiring of men whose qualifications and intelligence were inferior to her own.

Moreover, marriage to painter Max Maynard always was difficult. An alcoholic whose behaviour was erratic and irresponsible, he grew increasingly bitter and depressed over the years. Money was ever in short supply since Max had earned a Bachelor of Arts and throughout his university career would never receive adequate remuneration to support his family. Fredelle later described them as an "odd pair" (*Tree* 29) whose marriage lasted twenty-five years.

For Fredelle "a child represents a second chance at being a perfect person. Inevitably, there's pressure on the child to go farther, achieve more" (*Tree* 241). Unaware until much later of her motivation—since mothers identify more strongly with daughters than sons, "seeing them more as extensions of themselves.... Ego boundaries between mothers and daughters are more fluid, more undefined" (Hirsch, "Mothers" 183)—Fredelle encouraged her daughters to become writers, partly because writing was a skill she herself had found useful in establishing an alternate career, and because she and Max took "sensual pleasure" in language: "For them, language was music. They loved the sound of the human voice delivering the best the English language had to offer" (*At Home* 13). More significantly, for Fredelle, who married outside her faith and whose cultural link to Judaism diminished over time, mentoring served in place of faith and culture as a vital means of fostering her daughter's identity as a writer.

Although Fredelle does not describe her teaching methods, Joyce does:

> [I]n a circle of shabby furniture, surrounded by my father's paintings, my sister and I read our manuscripts aloud for our parents. With file cards and yellow legal pads in hand, they take notes and analyze, one line at a time, every metaphor and choice of adjective. They talk about the rhythm of our sentences, the syntax, the punctuation. My father is a careful and demanding editor, but my mother's criticism is the most exacting. Her instruction is incomparable.... (*At Home* 39-40)

Unlike Joyce, who casts Fredelle in the dual roles of teacher and nurturer to show how her mother's insistence on mentoring shaped their love, Fredelle focuses on her emotional relationship with her daughter. In her memoir, Fredelle does not distinguish between the practical and emotional sides of mothering and soon appropriates her daughter's pain as her own (*Tree* 163).

In an important chapter entitled "Two Daughters," Fredelle explores her connections with Rona and Joyce. Written in the form of two letters, Fredelle's most intimate voice is heard here. For her daughters she summons her "singing voice. It is the gift of life—of my rich lonely childhood, a marriage which forced me to confront my deepest feelings, *my suffering love for my children*, my experiences of failure" (*Tree* 134, italics mine). She writes to Joyce:

> Only in these last years have I begun to understand how I trained you to need me, because I needed you. Second child, second daughter, you were born when I had no more hopes for my marriage.... I loved you with a passion I did not then see as dangerous. You were the child who would redeem a disastrous marriage, gratify my parents, enrich and justify my life. (*Tree* 159-60)

Throughout *The Tree of Life* Fredelle seeks to be "truer" (xxi) to life and experience than she had been earlier in *Raisins and Almonds,* which she had come to regard as a sunnier, less authentic memoir (*Tree* xxi). A commitment to honesty—despite its attendant pain—is palpable in her words to Joyce. Fredelle writes as the woman who has given Joyce life, has mothered her, and prepared her for the writing life. Moreover, she writes as a woman bequeathing her "singing voice" (*Tree* 134) to the daughter she loves and on whom she has placed "her most ambitious expectations" (*At Home* 39).

In her letter to Joyce, Fredelle conflates facets of herself—mother, mentor, and writer—to interpret their abiding connection. A willing "rescuer," Fredelle has required that Joyce function as "rescuee" (*Tree* 166), poised to summon mother at will. Writing to her daughter in *The Tree of Life,* Fredelle comes to recognize the folly and cost of such interdependence and offers Joyce liberation. She writes with courage as she examines the ties that have bound her and Joyce, but does not relinquish those ties. Instead, she embraces a view of herself as imperfect mother and mentor and offers that self to her daughter.

In *At Home in the World* Joyce is determined "to tell the story of a real woman with all her flaws" (3). Like Fredelle—whose second volume of tough and honest (*Tree* xxi) memoirs appeared after her parents and ex-husband had died—Joyce's commitment to a true account of herself is possible only after the death of her parents. And, like Fredelle, in her work Joyce revisits and revises previous representations of people and events. In a prefatory note, she claims: "As painful as parts of this story may be, particularly to people who knew and loved my parents, I believe my mother and father would understand and even celebrate my having found, at last, the freedom to write as I do now" (*At Home* xiv). Joyce's narrative is framed by her parents, whom she invokes as spiritual overseers of her memoir. As Fredelle did earlier, Joyce acknowledges the blurring of boundaries between herself and her parents, a lifelong problem between "my mother and me ... [whose] view of all things ... has always been mine" (*At Home* 6, 113).

Joyce also inherited her mother's drive and ambition. From the age of twelve, she was "consumed with a desire to win contests, earn money, earn recognition from the world and, above all, from my parents" (*At Home* 41-42). Fredelle encouraged Joyce, much as her own mother fostered her development. Fredelle and Joyce describe Rona Bruser as having sought professional success for her two daughters. In spite of a traditional Jewish reverence for men—which led her to accept an impoverished life as wife to a loving but unsuccessful shopkeeper in a series of small Saskatchewan towns—she was "a woman of fierce ambition and pride in her children" (*At Home* 12). At a time when Jewish girls were raised to be wives and mothers, Rona Bruser—perhaps by default, since she had no sons of her own—"launched Freidele [later Fredelle] in the study of elocution, the oral presentation of poetry" (*At Home* 12). Fredelle's father would submit her poetry to local newspapers for publication. When later she went on to win scholarships that took her to the University of Manitoba, the University of Toronto, and Radcliffe, both parents knew education would lead Fredelle away from her roots, since few Jewish men of the time would marry a woman with a doctorate. Despite her anxiety, however, Rona Bruser celebrated her daughter's academic achievement and thereby freed her from the restrictive roles a traditional Jewish upbringing might encourage.

Joyce basked in similar encouragement. As a young adolescent, she joined her mother's meetings with students:

> I am so proud of my glorious, brilliant, funny, outrageous mother. I take in every word she tells her students about writing. In between these classes, I sit beside my mother on our couch when she's marking student papers, and read all her comments in the margins....
>
> By the time I'm twelve or thirteen, I've heard enough of my mother's comments that when one of her students reads a paper, I know just what she'll say. Everytime I sit down to write, I hear her voice. (*At Home* 20-21)

In addition to practical advice, Fredelle imparts her view of writing as valuable. The belief she shares with her daughter—that writing is one of life's most significant undertakings—is an inestimable gift meant to celebrate Joyce's abilities and enhance her confidence.

In fact, Joyce's success at age eighteen launched her career as writer. Her achievement was coloured, however, by ambivalent feelings: "With the publication of this article, I have not simply accomplished something for my own self. I have vindicated the sacrifices and the terrible disappointments my parents have suffered over the years" (*At Home* 69). Ironically, Fredelle's similar need to please her parents also took the form of academic success, publications, later marriage and children. Evidently, Joyce internalized Fredelle's belief that achievement belonged as much to her parents as herself.

Joyce was not alone in her ambivalence. As her daughter surpassed her greatest hopes, Fredelle felt shocked. A week following the *New York Times* publication, Fredelle wrote to Joyce who was a freshman at Yale University:

> I have thought of you a great deal this past week, with a mixture of feelings you can imagine: pride, love, anxiety, joy, excitement, apprehension. Also a certain startlement. I never doubted that you would achieve brilliant success, most probably in writing. I just didn't think it would happen so suddenly or so soon, and with such dramatic reverberations. Did we cast you on the tide? Were you ready to be cast? Where will the current carry you? I don't know, but the tide is moving…. (*At Home* 77)

Having schooled her from a young age, Fredelle took pleasure in Joyce's accomplishment. But daughter and mother both were unnerved by rapid success and the publicity it generated. The tone of Fredelle's letter suggests a mother who feels abandoned by the daughter she always has loved and needed, as she would admit later in *The Tree of Life*. Joyce, on the other hand, felt torn: proud but uncertain, confident but cautious. At the time of publication, she was a teenager who had been raised "deeply isolated in the insular world" (*At Home* 129) of family. In all likelihood, mother and daughter felt threatened by a success that soon would weaken the insularity and protection of family life.

Nancy Chodorow and Susan Contratto describe the psychological dyad of the mother and child as

> a unique and potent relationship.... It explains why mothers (even in their oppression by patriarchy) are so all-powerful in relation to their children, and why the mother-child relation is likely to be so bound up with powerful feelings. Mother and child are on a psychological desert island ... each is continually impinging and intruding on the other. (63)

Actually, "An 18-Year-Old Looks Back on Life" marked a division in the "unique and potent" relationship between Fredelle and Joyce. Soon they ceased to be partners: Fredelle's own writing career was established and Joyce began to consult with editors on writing projects. Moreover, Joyce was no longer tied to her bedroom at home in Durham, New Hampshire, once the only place she could settle herself to write. In fact, when given the assignment by the *New York Times*, she had returned home from Yale since

> All my life I have associated writing with my parents' house. Every entry I ever produced for the *Scholastic Magazine* contest was produced in my bedroom. Every time I finished writing something there, I would call to my parents. My father would make tea and my mother would set homemade cookies on a plate and wheel a teacart with the tea and cookies and cups into our living room. I would read out loud to them.... Finally they both agreed I had done my best, and my mother would type my work and mail it to the contest.
> When I learn that I have an assignment from *The New York Times*, I know that to be successful, I have to go back home to write. (*At Home* 63)

Soon, however, Joyce was writing magazine articles in a dormitory room at Yale and later in an apartment in New York. Less dependent on her mother for practical assistance, she nonetheless was bound to her emotionally. When, for example, her relationship ended with J. D. Salinger—his hypocrisy and caustic assessment of her parents confused and later angered Joyce—she sought the solace of Fredelle. If she no longer required her mother's advice on writing—how to write crisp, limpid prose; how to pitch ideas to editors; how to write for particular audiences—she still needed her mother "with the groping passion of that little girl lost" (Rich 225).

Joyce's adult relationship with Fredelle was "strained" (*At Home* 226), partly because as "life increasingly resembles my mother's, I find myself resenting her so deeply that it's now almost impossible for us to be together" (*At Home* 227). Joyce's own unhappy marriage and financial difficulties recalled those endured by Fredelle. By 1977, at the age of twenty-four, Joyce was married and soon pregnant with a daughter (born 1978). She and her husband, Steve Bethel, subsequently had two sons (born 1981 and 1984 respectively), as they struggled to maintain their household on her earnings as a writer and his as a painter. On her part, Fredelle was perplexed by her adult daughter and deliberately distanced herself from Joyce (*At Home* 251).

The confusion between parent and child had its roots in a relationship that early on melded mothering and mentoring. As the needs of mentor-protégée receded with maturity, the mother-daughter bond was altered irrevocably. Moreover, Fredelle came to relish the new independence of late middle age—she was now a practiced writer and content in a new relationship with Sydney Bacon—while Joyce came to reject "the teacher" and idealize "the mother," a fantasy of maternal perfection that "has led to the cultural oppression of women in the interest of a child whose needs are also fantasied" (Chodorow and Contratto 73). As Marianne Hirsch explains,

> The adult woman who is mother continues to exist only in relation to her child, never as a subject in her own right. And in her maternal function, she remains an object, always distanced, always idealized or denigrated, always mystified, always represented through the small child's point of view. (*Mother* 167)

In fact, the relationship between mother and adult daughter did not end once Joyce was launched in her own career. Rather, it transmuted into a connection based on similar personal circumstances. Ironically, but not surprisingly, when they reached an impasse in their love, Fredelle and Joyce sought to resolve their difficulties through writing.

Within the culture of patriarchy, it is extremely difficult to be either mother/mentor or daughter/protégée. Patriarchy requires and endorses passive mothering and continues to undermine a mother's desire for her daughter's autonomy. Herein lies the dilemma of a mother who would offer her daughter a practical education and a daughter who looks to her mother for unconditional and unending love. In New Hampshire of the 1950s, Fredelle Bruser Maynard—differentiated from the community of women by citizenship, religion, and education—undertook what Rich terms "courageous mothering" (246) which required "a strong sense of *self*-nurture in the mother" (245) herself. Fredelle's will to challenge convention and Jewish tradition—on her own behalf and that of her daughters—showed her remarkable ability and fortitude.

Rich elaborates: "The most important thing one woman can do for another is illuminate and expand her sense of actual possibilities. For a mother, this means ... trying to expand the limits of her life. *To refuse to be a victim*: and then to go on from there" (246). When the academy refused her entry, Fredelle sought professional opportunities elsewhere. Although eminently suited to a life of scholarship, she applied her hard-won skills to magazine writing and eventually became a respected journalist. Her volumes of memoirs attest to her wisdom and creativity, gifts that sustained her throughout life, as well as the value she finally attached to her Jewish inheritance. Under difficult personal circumstances, she first eked out and later earned a living that helped support her family. Her achievement was and remains significant.

By her own account, Joyce adored her mother "fiercely and deeply" (*At Home* xiv), and took pride in her brilliance and professional accomplishments. Their adult relationship was difficult, however, when Joyce could not acknowledge that daughters "need mothers who want their own freedom and ours" (Rich 247). In *At Home in the World*, Joyce regrets that her early work resonates with Fredelle's voice while I read that blending of writerly voices as a startling success for a young woman. Joyce had the benefit of a mother who struggled to articulate her own voice—and who sought to make that same struggle less arduous for her daughter. For

> [t]he quality of the mother's life—however embattled and unprotected—is her primary bequest to her daughter, because a woman who can believe in herself, who is a fighter, and who continues to struggle to create liveable space around her, is demonstrating to her daughter that these possibilities exist. (Rich 247)

Fredelle's "bequest" is Joyce's writerly voice, rich and sonorous with knowledge and experience of the past. That mother and daughter describe a troubled, often painful relationship is not surprising, given the gargantuan task Fredelle undertook in spite of patriarchal resistance to worldly education for girls and a religious tradition that prescribes restrictive roles for women. Fredelle came to accept the limitations of her role as mother and mentor and in *The Tree of Life* wrote to free her daughter from the bind of their relationship. Joyce, too, came to see that her life's work—writing—was a realization of her mother's wishes for her and a testimony to their love. If she had been raised differently, she admits in *At Home in the World*, "I might not possess the tools to tell this story" (xiv). The mutual validation of the mother-daughter bond returns Fredelle and Joyce to their Jewish inheritance, which honours familial relationships. Indeed, as mother and daughter who share love and success, they stand together—at odds with the world, free to relish their achievement.

## Notes

[1] Mothers and daughters who are both writers include Anita Desai and Kiran Desai; Florence Randal Livesay and Dorothy Livesay; Linda Spalding and Esta Spalding; Mary Wollstonecraft and Mary Shelley.
[2] For the sake of clarity, I refer simply to Fredelle and Joyce throughout this essay.
[3] Rona Maynard is former editor of *Chatelaine*, a magazine for

Canadian women. She has written of her own relationship with Fredelle in *My Mother's Daughter: A Memoir* (Toronto: McClelland and Stewart, 2007).

[4]Joyce Maynard's publications include *Looking Back: A Chronicle of Growing Up Old in the Sixties* (Garden City, NY: Doubleday, 1973); *Baby Love* (New York: Knopf, 1981); *Domestic Affairs: Enduring the Pleasures of Motherhood and Family Life* (New York: Time Books, 1987); *New House* (New York: Harcourt Brace Jovanovich, 1987); *To Die For* (New York: Dutton, 1992); *Where Love Goes* (New York: Crown Publishers, 1995); *At Home in the World: A Memoir* (New York: Picador, 1998); *The Usual Rules* (New York: St. Martin's Press, 2003); *The Cloud Chamber* (New York: Simon and Schuster, 2005); and *Internal Combustion: The Story of a Marriage and a Murder in the Motor City* (Somerset, NJ: Jossey-Bass, 2006).

[5]Fredelle Bruser Maynard's publications include *Raisins and Almonds* (Garden City, NY: Doubleday, 1972); *Guiding Your Child to a More Creative Life* (Garden City, NY: Doubleday, 1973); *The Child Care Crisis: The Real Costs of Day Care for You—and Your Child* (Markham, ON: Viking Penguin, 1985); and *The Tree of Life* (Markham, ON: Viking Penguin, 1988).

## Works Cited

Chodorow, Nancy, and Susan Contratto. "The Fantasy of the Perfect Mother." *Rethinking the Family: Some Feminist Questions*. Eds. Barrie Thorne with Marilyn Yalom. New York: Longman, 1982. 54-71.

Dunlop, Rishma. "Written on the Body." *Redefining Motherhood: Changing Identities and Patterns*. Eds. Sharon Abbey and Andrea O'Reilly. Toronto: Second Story Press, 1998. 103-24.

Hirsch, Marianne. *The Mother/Daughter Plot: Narrative, Psychoanalysis, Feminism*. Bloomington: Indiana University Press, 1989.

Hirsch, Marianne. "Mothers and Daughters." *Ties That Bind: Essays on Mothering and Patriarchy*. Eds. Jean F. O'Barr, Deborah Pope, and Mary Wyer. Chicago: University of Chicago Press, 1990. 177-99.

Lazar, David. "On Mentorship." *Ohio Review* 51 (1994): 25-33.

Maynard, Fredelle Bruser. *Raisins and Almonds*. Garden City, NY: Doubleday, 1972.

Maynard, Fredelle Bruser. *The Tree of Life*. Markham, ON: Viking Penguin, 1988.

Maynard, Joyce. "An 18-Year-Old Looks Back on Life." *New York Times Magazine* 23 April 1972: cover, 11, 76, 78-79, 82, 84-86.

Maynard, Joyce. *At Home in the World: A Memoir*. New York: Picador, 1998.

Rich, Adrienne. *Of Woman Born: Motherhood as Experience and Institution*. 1976. New York: Norton, 1995.

# Index

"An 18-Year-Old Looks Back on Life" (Joyce Maynard), 100, 106, 107
*At Home in the World* (Joyce Maynard), 99-110

*Basic Black with Pearls* (Weinzweig), 33, 39, 48; as cyclical, 53; and disguise/identity, 51-52; inconclusive ending of, 54; on marriage, 51-54; narrative form of, 51, 53; as psychotic, 51, 54, 59n3; and reality vs. illusion, 51-52, 53; writing of, 39-40
"The Bond" (Waddington), 81-82n1, 83
Bornstein, Eli, 38-39, 48
Bruser, Rona, 100, 105

*Canadian Jewish Short Stories* (ed. Waddington), 5, 7-8, 9
"A Classical Education" (Weinzweig), 40, 48
*Crackpot* (Wiseman), 77-81, 83-96; and affirmation of sexuality, 78-80; comedy/humour of, 79, 81, 87; family in, 77-78, 79, 87; as female-centred text, 77-78; garrulity/candour in, 5, 77, 78-79; identity in, 90-91; and incest, 78, 79-80, 84, 90, 95; narrative form of, 5; and prostitute as heroine, 77-81; and prostitute as mother, 78, 79, 83, 84, 88-91, 95, 96; and reinscription into Judaism, 81; as revisionist reading of *The Sacrifice*, 8, 73, 77, 81; and reward of love/marriage, 77, 80-81, 90-91; and subversion of patriarchal Judaism, 73, 77. *See also* Hoda

Eliot, George, 45
exile, 1, 5, 17-18, 23, 31, 93

*A Father and His Fate* (Compton-Burnett), 49
feminism, 3, 6-7, 48, 69

Gerber, Joanne, 61
Gold, Nora, 1, 2, 5, 8, 61-70; narrative form of, 61-62, 63; Zionism of, 61. *See also Marrow and Other Stories*
Gold, Nora, themes of: death, 67; emotional vs. physical self, 67-69; fantasy of romance, 67-68, 69-70; flawed/absent mothers,

66; identity, 63-64, 70; marriage, 63-64, 66-67, 69; miscarriage/stillbirth, 63; patriarchy of culture/relationships, 66-68, 69; patriarchy of Judaism, 61, 63, 65, 69; relationships outside marriage, 67, 68; sexual impropriety, 65-66; women in midlife, 62, 63-64, 69

Hebrew, 5, 63
Hoda (*Crackpot*), 5, 73, 77-81, 83-96; acceptance of, 88; exploitation of, 87; and "fall" into prostitution, 84-85, 86, 87; family of, 77-78, 79, 87; garrulity/candour of, 5, 77, 78-79; and incest, 77-78, 80, 84, 90, 95; isolation/vulnerability of, 88; as mother, 77, 78, 83, 84, 89-91, 95, 96; punishment/redemption of, 90-91; as reinscribed into Judaism, 80-81; as rewarded with love/marriage, 77, 80-81, 90-91. See also *Crackpot*
"The Homecoming" (Weinzweig), 48, 55
House of Anansi Press, 39
Howe, Fanny Quincy, 84, 85

identity, 6, 9; in *Crackpot* (Wiseman), 90-91; in Gold's work, 63-64, 69-70; in *The Singing Fire* (Nattel), 95-96; in Waddington's life/work, 7, 13, 17-18, 21-25, 28-31; in Weinzweig's life/work, 35-36, 51-52
Israel, 28-29, 61, 63, 65

Jewish Canadian women writers: and absence of critical tradition, 1, 2; and Canadian experience, 4; as feminists, 3, 6; and Judaism, 4, 6-7, 8, 9; mentorship of, 9, 16-17, 99-110; and morality, 5–6; and narrative form, 5; and quest for knowledge, 6; and sense of fragmentation, 2; thematic concerns of, 5–7; and writings in Yiddish, 2
Judaism: marriage outside, 9, 19-21, 26-27, 29; patriarchy of, 5, 6-7, 9, 61, 63, 64-65, 69, 73-77; and return to community/culture, 80-81, 93, 110; and women's education, 105, 109

Klein, A.M., 16-17
Korzen, Nehama (*The Singing Fire*), 4, 84, 86, 91-96; and adopted daughter, 94-96; exploitation/brutalization of, 92; and "fall" into prostitution, 83-84, 86, 92; marriage of, 93-94, 95-96; as mother figure, 9, 84, 92-96; punishment of, 84, 93; rescue/redemption of, 93-94; and return to Jewish community, 93; and unwed mother, 94-95, 96

Laiah (*The Sacrifice*): as challenging Judaic patriarchy/authority, 73, 76-77; and incest, 76, 80; murder/silencing of, 8, 73, 74, 76-77, 81; ostracism/punishment of, 73, 76-77

marriage: and adultery, 18-19, 25-26, 28-29; ceremony of, 49-50; as loving/forgiving, 93-94, 95-96; outside Judaism, 9, 19-21, 26-27, 28-29, 102-03; as stifling/unfulfilling, 5, 7, 8, 25-26, 51-54, 56, 57, 62; traditional, 7, 47, 51-54

*Marrow and Other Stories* (Gold), 61-70; "Final Movement," 66-67; "Flesh," 66, 67-68; "The Lesson of the Rabbi," 65-66; "Marrow," 63; "Miniatures," 63-65; "The Prayer," 6, 68-69; "Yosepha," 65, 66

Maynard, Fredelle Bruser, 2, 4; and daughter's early success, 106-07; education of, 102, 105; first memoir of, 99, 104; honesty of, 99, 104; and Judaism, 102-03, 105, 109, 110; marriage of, 102; mother of, 100, 105; as mother/mentor, 9, 99-110; as refused university post, 102, 109; second memoir of, 99-110; as teacher, 103, 105

Maynard, Joyce, 2, 4; as daughter/student, 9, 99-110; early article by, 100, 106, 107; honesty of, 100, 104-05; marriage of, 108; memoir of, 99-110; and reaction to early success, 106-07; and relationship with Salinger, 102, 107

Maynard, Max, 102

Maynard, Rona, 100, 103, 110n3

Maza, Ida, 16-17

Michaels, Anne, 1, 4

mother: as flawed/absent, 66-67; as mentor, 99-110; prostitute as, 9, 78, 79, 83-96; traditional, 7, 47, 52, 53, 91; unwed, 94-95, 96

mother-daughter relationship, 7, 9; in *Crackpot* (Wiseman), 77-78; in "Flesh" (Gold), 67-68; in *The Singing Fire* (Nattel), 94-96; of Weinzweig, 46, 47, 54-55; and writing vocation, 99, 110n1. *See also* Maynard, Fredelle Bruser; Maynard, Joyce

"My Mother's Luck" (Weinzweig), 40, 41, 46, 55

Nattel, Lilian, 2, 4. See also *The Singing Fire*

*Passing Ceremony* (Weinzweig), 33, 48-51; inconclusive ending of, 50; inspiration for, 38-39, 48; musical influence on, 48-49; narrative form of, 38-39, 48-49; as parody, 49-51; as psychotic, 59n3; publication of, 39, 48

Pinzer, Maimie: correspondence of, 84; and "fall" into prostitution, 86; as mother figure, 85-86, 96

Polk, James, 39

Pratt, E. J., 17

prostitute, Jewish, 5, 7, 9, 83, 84; in "The Bond" (Waddington), 81-82n1, 83; and life of Maimie Pinzer, 85-86, 96; as mother, 9, 78, 80, 83-96. *See also* Hoda (*Crackpot*); Korzen, Nehama (*The Singing Fire*); Laiah (*The Sacrifice*)

*Raisins and Almonds* (Fredelle Bruser Maynard), 99, 104

Richler, Mordecai, 3, 14

*The Sacrifice* (Wiseman): and challenges to Judaic patriarchy/authority, 6, 73, 74-77; and incest, 76, 80; as male-centred text, 73-74; and murder/silencing of prostitute, 8, 73, 74, 76-77, 81; and ostracism/punishment of sexuality, 73, 76-77; and patriarchy/misogyny of Judaism, 73-77; as revised by *Crackpot*, 8, 73, 77-78, 81; and silence/submission of women, 74, 76

Salinger, J. D., 102, 107

Scott, Duncan Campbell, 17

"The Sea at Bar" (Weinzweig), 42, 57

sexuality, female, 7, 9; affirmation of, 78-80; and exploitation/brutality, 92, 94, 95-96; ostracism/punishment of, 73, 76-77. *See also* marriage; prostitute, Jewish

*The Singing Fire* (Nattel), 84, 86, 91-96; identity in, 95-96; marriage in, 93-94, 95-96; narrative form of, 4; and prostitute as mother figure, 9, 84, 92-96; and return to Jewish community, 93; sexual exploitation/brutality in, 92, 94, 95-96; unwed mother in, 94-95, 96; and vicious cycle of prostitution, 94-96. *See also* Korzen, Nehama

*Summer at Lonely Beach and Other Stories* (Waddington), 13, 18-31; "Breaking Bread in Jerusalem," 28-30, 31; "Far from Snows of Winnipeg," 21-23, 27; "The Honeymoon House," 25-26, 28; "I'm Lonesome for Harrisburg," 31; "The Last Rehearsal," 23-25; "A Mixed Marriage," 19-21; "A Silence All Too Long," 26-28; "Summer at Lonely Beach," 18-19

"Surprise!" (Weinzweig), 38, 47

*The Tree of Life* (Fredelle Bruser Maynard), 99-104, 106, 110

*A View from the Roof* (Weinzweig), 33, 46, 48, 55-57; "Causation," 55, 56; "L'Envoi," 56; "The Homecoming," 55; "Journey to Porquis," 57; "The Means," 55-56; "My Mother's Luck," 46, 55; "A View from the Roof," 56-57; "What Happened to Ravel's Bolero?," 57

Waddington, Miriam, 1, 4-5, 13-31; childhood and education of, 13-18; on Jewish Canadian writing, 5, 7-8, 9; on identity, 6, 9, 13, 17-18, 31; mentor of, 16-17; poetry of, 13, 15–17, 81-82n1, 83; racism toward, 14-15, 17-18; short stories of, 7-8, 13; and socialism, 14, 31; at university, 17; and Yiddish language/writing, 14, 16, 18, 29, 31. *See also Summer at Lonely Beach and Other Stories*

Waddington, Miriam, themes of: adolescent awareness/discovery, 19-21; behavioural codes/conventions, 19, 20-21; class differences, 20; dislocation, 18, 23, 27; identity, 6, 13, 21-25, 28-30; Judaism/Jewish culture, 21-26, 28-30; marriage/relationships outside Judaism, 18-21, 26-27, 28-29; personal renewal, 25-30; prostitution, 81-82n1, 83; racism, 24; relationships outside marriage, 18-19, 25-26, 28-29

Weinzweig, Helen, 1-2, 4, 5, 8, 33-42; childhood and education of, 33, 34-35, 45-46; drama of, 40-41, 48, 55; early reading of, 34, 35; father of, 33, 40, 41, 45-46; and first-person narrative, 35, 51; first publication of, 38, 47; and husband's career/music, 33, 36-37, 47 48-49, 57; on identity, 35-36; inconclusive endings of, 50, 54, 57-58; late writing career of, 3, 33-34, 45, 47, 58; marginalization of, 45; marriage and family of, 33, 36-37, 47; mother of, 33, 40, 45-46, 47, 54-55; narrative form of, 33, 38-39, 41-42, 45, 48-49, 51, 53, 55; and novel in progress, 33, 41-42; novels of, 38-40, 45, 48; short stories of, 33, 38, 46, 47, 55-57; on style, 39, 41; on women's roles, 35-36; and Yiddish language/writing, 40, 46, 54-55. See also *Basic Black with Pearls*; *Passing Ceremony*; *A View from the Roof*

Weinzweig, Helen, themes of: art and music, 55, 57; disguise/identity, 52; marriage, 51-54, 55, 57; marriage ceremony, 49-51; memory, 55-56, 57; reality vs. illusion, 51-52, 53-54; relationships, 56-57; war experiences, 56, 57

Weinzweig, John, 34, 36-37, 46, 47, 57; twelve-tone music of, 33, 36, 57

Winnipeg, 67; in *Crackpot* (Wiseman), 83, 88; in Waddington's life/work, 13-14, 17, 19, 20, 22, 27, 29

Wiseman, Adele, 1, 3, 4-5; and female subject, in patriarchal culture of Judaism, 73-81. See also *Crackpot*; *The Sacrifice*

Yiddish, 2, 5, 92; in Waddington's life/work, 14, 16, 18, 29, 31; in Weinzweig's life/work, 40, 46, 54-55

*Photo: Gary Gottlieb*

Ruth Panofsky is Professor of English at Ryerson University in Toronto. She is the author of *The Force of Vocation: The Literary Career of Adele Wiseman*. Her poetry book, *Laike and Nahum: A Poem in Two Voices*, received the 2008 Canadian Jewish Book Award for Poetry.